Legal Self-Help Guide

Estate Planning
Organizer

Legal Self-Help Guide

Estate Planning
Organizer

Sanket Mistry, JD, MIA, edited by J.T. Levine, JD, MFA

Peerless Legal

ISBN 13: 978-1-940788-13-5
ISBN 10: 1-940788-13-7

Mistry, Sanket
Estate Planning Organizer: Legal Self-Help Guide
First Edition
Peerless Legal | Roanoke, Virginia | www.PeerlessLegal.com

™ and Peerless Legal are trademarks of PeerlessLegal.com.

Peerless Legal books are available for special promotions. For details, contact Peerless Legal by email at sales@peerlesslegal.com, or visit www.PeerlessLegal.com.

While the author has made every effort to provide accurate telephone numbers and internet addresses at the time of publication, neither the publisher nor author assume any responsibility for errors or changes that occur after publication. The publisher does not have any control over, and does not assume any responsibility for, author or third-party websites or their content.

This publication is designed to provide accurate and authoritative information in regard to the subject matters covered. It is sold with the understanding that the publisher and author are not engaged in rendering legal, accounting, or other professional services. If legal advice or other expert assistance is required, the services of a competent professional should be sought.

From a *Declaration of Principles jointly adopted by a Committee of the American Bar Association and a Committee of Publishers*

THIS PRODUCT IS NOT A SUBSITUTE FOR LEGAL ADVICE.
Disclaimer required by Texas statutes.

DISCLAIMER

Laws change constantly. Every effort has been made to provide the most up-to-date information. However, the author, publisher, and any and all persons or entities involved in any way in the preparation, publication, sale, or distribution of this publication disclaim any and all representations or warranties, express or implied, about the outcome or methods of use of this publication, and assume no liability for claims, losses, or damages arising from the use or misuse of this publication. All responsibilities for legal effects or consequences of any document prepared from, or action taken in reliance upon information contained in this publication are disclaimed. The reader should not rely on this author or this publisher for any professional advice. Users of this publication intending to use this publication for preparation of legal documents are advised to check specifically on the current, applicable laws in any jurisdiction in which they intend the documents to be effective. Make sure you are using the most recent edition.

What Is The Legal Self-Help Guide?

The Peerless Legal mission is to empower individuals by giving them legal self-help tools. The Legal Self-Help Guide series was created as the embodiment of that mission.

The goal of this Guide is to provide you with the information you need to get your estate planning documents in order. In doing so, we hope you will decide to plan your estate or know enough to feel confident in your decision to hire a licensed attorney. This Guide provides a meaningful alternative to most of the books in law libraries or provided by law firms. Peerless Legal's goal is for you to be able to understand this material so you can have important comprehensive information available to your loved ones and/or executor.

In this Guide, Peerless Legal provides you a way to organize your estate planning records to help you either create your own estate plan or be organized when you meet with your attorney who will plan your estate. This book is for you if:

- you want to organize your important information into one place,

- you want to prepare to create your own will,

- you have retained an attorney and want to be organized for the meeting,

- or you want to know more what all is included in an estate plan.

It is important to manage expectations when acting on your own behalf or with an attorney. The forms in this book are not legal documents and are meant only to help you organize your estate. There are no explanations, but most, if not all, of the forms require almost not explanations. Your needs may differ and all of the forms may not apply to you or your situation.

Warning There are some legal issues that seem simple and straight forward, but in reality only an attorney with extensive experience on the issue would know there is an inner-tangling.**

About the Author

Sanket Mistry earned his JD from the Walter F. George School of Law at Mercer University. He is a member of the New York State Bar and author of several books in the Legal Self-Help Guide series. He has worked, and volunteered, at a number of nonprofits, government agencies, and for-profit corporations. He also holds a BA in philosophy from Emory University and an MIA from Columbia University. He is an avid traveler and tennis player.

About the Editor

J.T. Levine earned her JD from the Walter F. George School of Law at Mercer University. She has edited several books for Peerless Legal. She is a member of the Georgia Bar. Prior to law school, she earned an MFA in Professional Writing from the Savannah College of Art and Design and a BA from the University of Miami. She is an animal lover and has a pharaoh hound named Tut.

Table of Contents

INTRODUCTION

ESTATE PLANNING ORGANIZER COVER PAGE

1. People
- A. My Information
- B. Beneficiaries
- C. Guardians for Minor Child
- D. Pets
- E. Others Who Depend On Me
- F. Witnesses and Notary Public
- G. Executor
- H. Trustees

2. Property
- A. Real Estate
- B. Bank Accounts
- C. Insurance and Annuities
- D. Death Benefits
- E. Trusts
- F. Non-Real Estate Debt
- G. Retirement Accounts and Pensions

3. Other Things
- A. Organ, Tissue, and Body Donation
- B. Inform the World of Your Death
  - a) Cremation or Burial, and Funeral and Memorial Services
  - b) Newspaper Obituary Information
- C. Other Notes

Introduction

This book will help you get your estate in order so that you can successfully create your own legal estate documents. This book is not intended to be read as a novel. It is intended to be used as a fill in the blank reference guide to help you plan your estate records. Pay attention to headings because they are your guide-posts. This book is laid out in a way to help you get organized quickly.

By the time you finish reading this book, you should have:

• successfully compiled your estate planning records into one place,

• an idea of the kinds of stuff you will leave behind, and

• understand the importance of having an estate plan.

The book contains a vast array of personal information. The information is a broad overview. Not every piece of information will pertain to you. Complete only those sections you feel comfortable completing. The tools in this book will assist you with gathering your personal information.

After you have created the sample forms in this book that apply to you and your situation, you should keep the documents together, preferably with the rest of your estate documents. The packet can become part of your estate. The packet will be helpful not only to your attorney (if you choose to retain one), but also to your executor who will help bring your final arrangements together following your death.

Note: since these documents contain highly sensitive information, take care to keep the records as private as possible.

Estate Planning Organizer

Cover Page

Name: _____   Date: _____

I have organized the following records:

1. People
- ❑ A. My Information
- ❑ B. Beneficiaries
- ❑ C. Guardians for Minor Child(ren)
- ❑ D. Pets
- ❑ E. Others Who Depend on Me
- ❑ F. Witnesses and Notary Public
- ❑ G. Executor
- ❑ H. Trustees

2. Property
- ❑ A. Real Estate
- ❑ B. Bank Accounts
- ❑ C. Insurance and Annuities
- ❑ D. Death Benefits
- ❑ E. Trusts
- ❑ F. Non-Real Estate Debt
- ❑ G. Retirement Accounts and Pensions

3. Other Things
- ❑ A. Organ, Tissue, and Body Donation
-    B. Inform the World of Your Death
  - ❑ a) Cremation or Burial, and Funeral and Memorial Services
  - ❑ b) Newspaper Obituary Information-

I have completed the following documents:

1. Wills
- ❑ Last Will and Testament
- ❑ Self-Proving Affidavit
- ❑ Living Will
- ❑ Amendment
- ❑ Revocation
- ❑ Ethical Will
- ❑ Explanation Letter

2. Power of Attorney
- ❑ Healthcare—Durable
- ❑ Financial—Durable
- ❑ Minor Child Care—Limited
- ❑ Revocation

3. Trusts
Living Trust: (select one)
- ❑ Simple One Person
- ❑ Simple Shared
- ❑ AB (With Disclaimer Statement: ❑No ❑Yes)
- ❑ Florida Witness Statement
- ❑ Assignment of Property to a Living Trust
- ❑ Affidavit of Assumption of Duties by Successor Trustee
- ❑ Amendment
- ❑ Revocation

1. People

A. My Information

Full legal (and maiden) name: _____

Address: _____

SSN: _____ DOB: _____ Phone: _____

I have a: Location:

   ❑ Birth certificate   _____

   ❑ Adoption papers   _____

   ❑ Social Security card   _____

   ❑ Driver's license   _____

   ❑ Passport   (Country_____) _____

   ❑ Divorce papers   _____

   ❑ Stocks   _____

   ❑ Bonds   _____

   ❑ Certificate of Deposits _____

   ❑ _____   _____

   ❑ _____   _____

   ❑ _____   _____

E-mail address: _____@_____ Password: _____

E-mail address: _____@_____ Password: _____

Social media: ❑ Facebook Username: _____ Password: _____

   ❑ _____ Username: _____ Password: _____

   ❑ _____ Username: _____ Password: _____

Armed Forces: ❑ No ❑ Yes, branch/unit: _____

_____ V.A. claims number: _____

Discharge: ❑ Active ❑ Retired ❑ Other: _____

Education: _____

_____

_____

_____

Diseases/illness/allergies that your doctors/family should know about: _____

_____

Doctor's name: Dr._____ Phone: _____

Address: _____

Past two years tax returns and W-2s located: _____

Employers for past five years:

Organization name: _____ Phone: _____

Contact Person (name and title): _____

Address: _____

Dates of employment: _____ to _____ ❑ F/T ❑ P/T

Organization name: _____ Phone: _____

Contact Person (name and title): _____

Address: _____

Dates of employment: _____ to _____ ❑ F/T ❑ P/T

Organization name: _____ Phone: _____

Contact Person (name and title): _____

Address: _____

Dates of employment: _____ to _____ ❏ F/T ❏ P/T

Organization name: _____ Phone: _____

Contact Person (name and title): _____

Address: _____

Dates of employment: _____ to _____ ❏ F/T ❏ P/T

Mother's name (and maiden name): _____

Year of birth: _____ Place of birth: _____ Number of children: ____

Deceased: ❏ No ❏ Yes, cause: _____ Number of marriages: __

Family medical history: _____

_____

Ancestor information: _____

_____

Father's name: _____

Year of birth: _____ Place of birth: _____ Number of children: ____

Deceased: ❏ No ❏ Yes, cause: _____ Number of marriages: __

Family medical history: _____

_____

Ancestor information: _____

_____

B. Beneficiaries (including people and charitable organizations)

Type (select one): ❑ Primary ❑ Alternate Primary ❑ Residuary ❑ Alternate Residuary

Beneficiary name: _____ Phone: _____

Address: _____

Relation: _____ Description of property to be left: _____

_____

Location of property: _____

Property given by (select one): ❑ Will ❑ Trust ❑ Gift ❑ Other: _____

Shared: ❑ No ❑ Yes, percentage given: _____% shared with: _____

_____

Type (select one): ❑ Primary ❑ Alternate Primary ❑ Residuary ❑ Alternate Residuary

Beneficiary name: _____ Phone: _____

Address: _____

Relation: _____ Description of property to be left: _____

_____

Location of property: _____

Property given by (select one): ❑ Will ❑ Trust ❑ Gift ❑ Other: _____

Shared: ❑ No ❑ Yes, percentage given: _____% shared with: _____

_____

Type (select one): ❑ Primary ❑ Alternate Primary ❑ Residuary ❑ Alternate Residuary

Beneficiary name: _____ Phone: _____

Address: _____

Relation: _____ Description of property to be left: _____

_____

Location of property: _____

Property given by (select one): ❑ Will ❑ Trust ❑ Gift ❑ Other: _____

Shared: ❑ No ❑ Yes, percentage given: _____% shared with: _____

_____

Type (select one): ❑ Primary ❑ Alternate Primary ❑ Residuary ❑ Alternate Residuary

Beneficiary name: _____ Phone: _____

Address: _____

Relation: _____ Description of property to be left: _____

_____

Location of property: _____

Property given by (select one): ❑ Will ❑ Trust ❑ Gift ❑ Other: _____

Shared: ❑ No ❑ Yes, percentage given: _____% shared with: _____

_____

Type (select one): ❏ Primary ❏ Alternate Primary ❏ Residuary ❏ Alternate Residuary

Beneficiary name: _____ Phone: _____

Address: _____

Relation: _____ Description of property to be left: _____

_____

Location of property: _____

Property given by (select one): ❏ Will ❏ Trust ❏ Gift ❏ Other: _____

Shared: ❏ No ❏ Yes, percentage given: _____% shared with: _____

_____

Type (select one): ❏ Primary ❏ Alternate Primary ❏ Residuary ❏ Alternate Residuary

Beneficiary name: _____ Phone: _____

Address: _____

Relation: _____ Description of property to be left: _____

_____

Location of property: _____

Property given by (select one): ❏ Will ❏ Trust ❏ Gift ❏ Other: _____

Shared: ❏ No ❏ Yes, percentage given: _____% shared with: _____

_____

Type (select one): ❑ Primary ❑ Alternate Primary ❑ Residuary ❑ Alternate Residuary

Beneficiary name: _____ Phone: _____

Address: _____

Relation: _____ Description of property to be left: _____

_____

Location of property: _____

Property given by (select one): ❑ Will ❑ Trust ❑ Gift ❑ Other: _____

Shared: ❑ No ❑ Yes, percentage given: _____% shared with: _____

_____

Type (select one): ❑ Primary ❑ Alternate Primary ❑ Residuary ❑ Alternate Residuary

Beneficiary name: _____ Phone: _____

Address: _____

Relation: _____ Description of property to be left: _____

_____

Location of property: _____

Property given by (select one): ❑ Will ❑ Trust ❑ Gift ❑ Other: _____

Shared: ❑ No ❑ Yes, percentage given: _____% shared with: _____

_____

Type (select one): ❑ Primary ❑ Alternate Primary ❑ Residuary ❑ Alternate Residuary

Beneficiary name: _____ Phone: _____

Address: _____

Relation: _____ Description of property to be left: _____

_____

Location of property: _____

Property given by (select one): ❑ Will ❑ Trust ❑ Gift ❑ Other: _____

Shared: ❑ No ❑ Yes, percentage given: _____% shared with: _____

_____

Type (select one): ❑ Primary ❑ Alternate Primary ❑ Residuary ❑ Alternate Residuary

Beneficiary name: _____ Phone: _____

Address: _____

Relation: _____ Description of property to be left: _____

_____

Location of property: _____

Property given by (select one): ❑ Will ❑ Trust ❑ Gift ❑ Other: _____

Shared: ❑ No ❑ Yes, percentage given: _____% shared with: _____

_____

Type (select one): ❑ Primary ❑ Alternate Primary ❑ Residuary ❑ Alternate Residuary

Beneficiary name: _____ Phone: _____

Address: _____

Relation: _____ Description of property to be left: _____

_____

Location of property: _____

Property given by (select one): ❑ Will ❑ Trust ❑ Gift ❑ Other: _____

Shared: ❑ No ❑ Yes, percentage given: _____% shared with: _____

_____

Type (select one): ❑ Primary ❑ Alternate Primary ❑ Residuary ❑ Alternate Residuary

Beneficiary name: _____ Phone: _____

Address: _____

Relation: _____ Description of property to be left: _____

_____

Location of property: _____

Property given by (select one): ❑ Will ❑ Trust ❑ Gift ❑ Other: _____

Shared: ❑ No ❑ Yes, percentage given: _____% shared with: _____

_____

Type (select one): ❑ Primary ❑ Alternate Primary ❑ Residuary ❑ Alternate Residuary

Beneficiary name: _____ Phone: _____

Address: _____

Relation: _____ Description of property to be left: _____

_____

Location of property: _____

Property given by (select one): ❑ Will ❑ Trust ❑ Gift ❑ Other: _____

Shared: ❑ No ❑ Yes, percentage given: _____% shared with: _____

_____

Type (select one): ❑ Primary ❑ Alternate Primary ❑ Residuary ❑ Alternate Residuary

Beneficiary name: _____ Phone: _____

Address: _____

Relation: _____ Description of property to be left: _____

_____

Location of property: _____

Property given by (select one): ❑ Will ❑ Trust ❑ Gift ❑ Other: _____

Shared: ❑ No ❑ Yes, percentage given: _____% shared with: _____

_____

Type (select one): ❑ Primary ❑ Alternate Primary ❑ Residuary ❑ Alternate Residuary

Beneficiary name: _____ Phone: _____

Address: _____

Relation: _____ Description of property to be left: _____

_____

Location of property: _____

Property given by (select one): ❑ Will ❑ Trust ❑ Gift ❑ Other: _____

Shared: ❑ No ❑ Yes, percentage given: _____% shared with: _____

_____

Type (select one): ❑ Primary ❑ Alternate Primary ❑ Residuary ❑ Alternate Residuary

Beneficiary name: _____ Phone: _____

Address: _____

Relation: _____ Description of property to be left: _____

_____

Location of property: _____

Property given by (select one): ❑ Will ❑ Trust ❑ Gift ❑ Other: _____

Shared: ❑ No ❑ Yes, percentage given: _____% shared with: _____

_____

Type (select one): ❑ Primary ❑ Alternate Primary ❑ Residuary ❑ Alternate Residuary

Beneficiary name: _____ Phone: _____

Address: _____

Relation: _____ Description of property to be left: _____

_____

Location of property: _____

Property given by (select one): ❑ Will ❑ Trust ❑ Gift ❑ Other: _____

Shared: ❑ No ❑ Yes, percentage given: _____% shared with: _____

_____

Type (select one): ❑ Primary ❑ Alternate Primary ❑ Residuary ❑ Alternate Residuary

Beneficiary name: _____ Phone: _____

Address: _____

Relation: _____ Description of property to be left: _____

_____

Location of property: _____

Property given by (select one): ❑ Will ❑ Trust ❑ Gift ❑ Other: _____

Shared: ❑ No ❑ Yes, percentage given: _____% shared with: _____

_____

Type (select one): ❑ Primary ❑ Alternate Primary ❑ Residuary ❑ Alternate Residuary

Beneficiary name: _____ Phone: _____

Address: _____

Relation: _____ Description of property to be left: _____

_____

Location of property: _____

Property given by (select one): ❑ Will ❑ Trust ❑ Gift ❑ Other: _____

Shared: ❑ No ❑ Yes, percentage given: _____% shared with: _____

_____

Type (select one): ❑ Primary ❑ Alternate Primary ❑ Residuary ❑ Alternate Residuary

Beneficiary name: _____ Phone: _____

Address: _____

Relation: _____ Description of property to be left: _____

_____

Location of property: _____

Property given by (select one): ❑ Will ❑ Trust ❑ Gift ❑ Other: _____

Shared: ❑ No ❑ Yes, percentage given: _____% shared with: _____

_____

Type (select one): ❑ Primary ❑ Alternate Primary ❑ Residuary ❑ Alternate Residuary

Beneficiary name: _____ Phone: _____

Address: _____

Relation: _____ Description of property to be left: _____

_____

Location of property: _____

Property given by (select one): ❑ Will ❑ Trust ❑ Gift ❑ Other: _____

Shared: ❑ No ❑ Yes, percentage given: _____% shared with: _____

_____

Type (select one): ❑ Primary ❑ Alternate Primary ❑ Residuary ❑ Alternate Residuary

Beneficiary name: _____ Phone: _____

Address: _____

Relation: _____ Description of property to be left: _____

_____

Location of property: _____

Property given by (select one): ❑ Will ❑ Trust ❑ Gift ❑ Other: _____

Shared: ❑ No ❑ Yes, percentage given: _____% shared with: _____

_____

C. Guardians for Minor Child

Child's name: _____ Phone: _____

Address: _____

DOB: _____ SSN: _____ Relation: _____

Important documents located: _____

Any trust(s): ☐ No ☐ Yes, trust(s) name(s): _____

    Property held in trust: _____

Property not held in trust: _____

Doctor's name: Dr. _____ Phone: _____

    Address: _____

Special needs/allergies: _____

Personal guardian name: _____ Phone: _____

    Address: _____

Alternate personal guardian: _____ Phone: _____

    Address: _____

Property manager: ☐ No ☐ Yes, name: _____ Phone: _____

    Address: _____

Child's name: _____ Phone: _____

Address: _____

DOB: _____ SSN: _____ Relation: _____

Important documents located: _____

Any trust(s): ❑ No ❑ Yes, trust(s) name(s): _____

      Property held in trust: _____

Property not held in trust: _____

Doctor's name: Dr. _____ Phone: _____

      Address: _____

Special needs/allergies: _____

Personal guardian name: _____ Phone: _____

      Address: _____

Alternate personal guardian: _____ Phone: _____

      Address: _____

Property manager: ❑ No ❑ Yes, name: _____ Phone: _____

      Address: _____

Child's name: _____ Phone: _____

Address: _____

DOB: _____ SSN: _____ Relation: _____

Important documents located: _____

Any trust(s): ❑ No ❑ Yes, trust(s) name(s): _____

      Property held in trust: _____

Property not held in trust: _____

Doctor's name: Dr. _____ Phone: _____

      Address: _____

Special needs/allergies: _____

Personal guardian name: _____ Phone: _____

      Address: _____

Alternate personal guardian: _____ Phone: _____

      Address: _____

Property manager: ❑ No ❑ Yes, name: _____ Phone: _____

      Address: _____

Child's name: _____ Phone: _____

Address: _____

DOB: _____ SSN: _____ Relation: _____

Important documents located: _____

Any trust(s): ❑ No ❑ Yes, trust(s) name(s): _____

     Property held in trust: _____

Property not held in trust: _____

Doctor's name: Dr. _____ Phone: _____

     Address: _____

Special needs/allergies: _____

Personal guardian name: _____ Phone: _____

     Address: _____

Alternate personal guardian: _____ Phone: _____

     Address: _____

Property manager: ❑ No ❑ Yes, name: _____ Phone: _____

     Address: _____

Child's name: _____ Phone: _____

Address: _____

DOB: _____ SSN: _____ Relation: _____

Important documents located: _____

Any trust(s): ❑ No ❑ Yes, trust(s) name(s): _____

    Property held in trust: _____

Property not held in trust: _____

Doctor's name: Dr. _____ Phone: _____

    Address: _____

Special needs/allergies: _____

Personal guardian name: _____ Phone: _____

    Address: _____

Alternate personal guardian: _____ Phone: _____

    Address: _____

Property manager: ❑ No ❑ Yes, name: _____ Phone: _____

    Address: _____

D. Pets

Animal name: _____ Age: _____ Species: _____

Color(s)/marking(s)/distinction(s): _____

Spayed/neutered: ❑ No ❑ Yes   Diet/medication(s): _____

Shot(s)/license/important documents located: _____

Veterinarian name: Dr._____ Phone: _____

        Address: _____

New owner name: _____ Phone: _____

        Address: _____

Alternate name: _____ Phone: _____

        Address: _____

Other instructions: _____

Animal name: _____ Age: _____ Species: _____

Color(s)/marking(s)/distinction(s): _____

Spayed/neutered: ❑ No ❑ Yes   Diet/medication(s): _____

Shot(s)/license/important documents located: _____

Veterinarian name: Dr._____ Phone: _____

        Address: _____

New owner name: _____ Phone: _____

        Address: _____

Alternate name: _____ Phone: _____

        Address: _____

Other instructions: _____

Animal name: _____ Age: _____ Species: _____

Color(s)/marking(s)/distinction(s): _____

Spayed/neutered: ❑ No ❑ Yes   Diet/medication(s): _____

Shot(s)/license/important documents located: _____

Veterinarian name: Dr._____ Phone: _____

Address: _____

New owner name: _____ Phone: _____

Address: _____

Alternate name: _____ Phone: _____

Address: _____

Other instructions: _____

Animal name: _____ Age: _____ Species: _____

Color(s)/marking(s)/distinction(s): _____

Spayed/neutered: ❑ No ❑ Yes   Diet/medication(s): _____

Shot(s)/license/important documents located: _____

Veterinarian name: Dr._____ Phone: _____

Address: _____

New owner name: _____ Phone: _____

Address: _____

Alternate name: _____ Phone: _____

Address: _____

Other instructions: _____

Animal name: _____ Age: _____ Species: _____

Color(s)/marking(s)/distinction(s): _____

Spayed/neutered: ❑ No ❑ Yes   Diet/medication(s): _____

Shot(s)/license/important documents located: _____

Veterinarian name: Dr._____ Phone: _____

        Address: _____

New owner name: _____ Phone: _____

        Address: _____

Alternate name: _____ Phone: _____

        Address: _____

Other instructions: _____

Animal name: _____ Age: _____ Species: _____

Color(s)/marking(s)/distinction(s): _____

Spayed/neutered: ❑ No ❑ Yes   Diet/medication(s): _____

Shot(s)/license/important documents located: _____

Veterinarian name: Dr._____ Phone: _____

        Address: _____

New owner name: _____ Phone: _____

        Address: _____

Alternate name: _____ Phone: _____

        Address: _____

Other instructions: _____

E.   Others Who Depend On Me

Name: _____ Phone: _____

Address: _____

Relation: _____ Location of documents: _____

Doctor's name: Dr. _____ Phone: _____

     Address: _____

Special needs/allergies: _____

Personal guardian name: _____ Phone: _____

     Address: _____

Alternate personal guardian: _____ Phone: _____

     Address: _____

Name: _____ Phone: _____

Address: _____

Relation: _____ Location of documents: _____

Doctor's name: Dr. _____ Phone: _____

     Address: _____

Special needs/allergies: _____

Personal guardian name: _____ Phone: _____

     Address: _____

Alternate personal guardian: _____ Phone: _____

     Address: _____

Name: _____ Phone: _____

Address: _____

Relation: _____ Location of documents: _____

Doctor's name: Dr. _____ Phone: _____

    Address: _____

Special needs/allergies: _____

Personal guardian name: _____ Phone: _____

    Address: _____

Alternate personal guardian: _____ Phone: _____

    Address: _____

Name: _____ Phone: _____

Address: _____

Relation: _____ Location of documents: _____

Doctor's name: Dr. _____ Phone: _____

    Address: _____

Special needs/allergies: _____

Personal guardian name: _____ Phone: _____

    Address: _____

Alternate personal guardian: _____ Phone: _____

    Address: _____

Name: _____ Phone: _____

Address: _____

Relation: _____ Location of documents: _____

Doctor's name: Dr. _____ Phone: _____

    Address: _____

Special needs/allergies: _____

Personal guardian name: _____ Phone: _____

    Address: _____

Alternate personal guardian: _____ Phone: _____

    Address: _____

Name: _____ Phone: _____

Address: _____

Relation: _____ Location of documents: _____

Doctor's name: Dr. _____ Phone: _____

    Address: _____

Special needs/allergies: _____

Personal guardian name: _____ Phone: _____

    Address: _____

Alternate personal guardian: _____ Phone: _____

    Address: _____

Name: _____ Phone: _____

Address: _____

Relation: _____ Location of documents: _____

Doctor's name: Dr. _____ Phone: _____

      Address: _____

Special needs/allergies: _____

Personal guardian name: _____ Phone: _____

      Address: _____

Alternate personal guardian: _____ Phone: _____

      Address: _____

Name: _____ Phone: _____

Address: _____

Relation: _____ Location of documents: _____

Doctor's name: Dr. _____ Phone: _____

      Address: _____

Special needs/allergies: _____

Personal guardian name: _____ Phone: _____

      Address: _____

Alternate personal guardian: _____ Phone: _____

      Address: _____

Name: _____ Phone: _____

Address: _____

Relation: _____ Location of documents: _____

Doctor's name: Dr. _____ Phone: _____

        Address: _____

Special needs/allergies: _____

Personal guardian name: _____ Phone: _____

        Address: _____

Alternate personal guardian: _____ Phone: _____

        Address: _____

Name: _____ Phone: _____

Address: _____

Relation: _____ Location of documents: _____

Doctor's name: Dr. _____ Phone: _____

        Address: _____

Special needs/allergies: _____

Personal guardian name: _____ Phone: _____

        Address: _____

Alternate personal guardian: _____ Phone: _____

        Address: _____

F. Witnesses and Notary Public

Type (select one): ☐ Witness ☐ Notary Public (name of business: _____)

Name: _____ Phone: _____

Address: _____

Document(s) to which they are acting: _____

_____

Type (select one): ☐ Witness ☐ Notary Public (name of business: _____)

Name: _____ Phone: _____

Address: _____

Document(s) to which they are acting: _____

_____

Type (select one): ☐ Witness ☐ Notary Public (name of business: _____)

Name: _____ Phone: _____

Address: _____

Document(s) to which they are acting: _____

_____

Type (select one): ☐ Witness ☐ Notary Public (name of business: _____)

Name: _____ Phone: _____

Address: _____

Document(s) to which they are acting: _____

_____

Type (select one): ❑ Witness ❑ Notary Public (name of business: _____)

Name: _____ Phone: _____

Address: _____

Document(s) to which they are acting: _____

_____

Type (select one): ❑ Witness ❑ Notary Public (name of business: _____)

Name: _____ Phone: _____

Address: _____

Document(s) to which they are acting: _____

_____

Type (select one): ❑ Witness ❑ Notary Public (name of business: _____)

Name: _____ Phone: _____

Address: _____

Document(s) to which they are acting: _____

_____

Type (select one): ❑ Witness ❑ Notary Public (name of business: _____)

Name: _____ Phone: _____

Address: _____

Document(s) to which they are acting: _____

_____

Type (select one): ❏ Witness ❏ Notary Public (name of business: _____)

Name: _____ Phone: _____

Address: _____

Document(s) to which they are acting: _____

_____

Type (select one): ❏ Witness ❏ Notary Public (name of business: _____)

Name: _____ Phone: _____

Address: _____

Document(s) to which they are acting: _____

_____

Type (select one): ❏ Witness ❏ Notary Public (name of business: _____)

Name: _____ Phone: _____

Address: _____

Document(s) to which they are acting: _____

_____

Type (select one): ❏ Witness ❏ Notary Public (name of business: _____)

Name: _____ Phone: _____

Address: _____

Document(s) to which they are acting: _____

_____

Type (select one): ❑ Witness ❑ Notary Public (name of business: _____)

Name: _____ Phone: _____

Address: _____

Document(s) to which they are acting: _____

_____

Type (select one): ❑ Witness ❑ Notary Public (name of business: _____)

Name: _____ Phone: _____

Address: _____

Document(s) to which they are acting: _____

_____

Type (select one): ❑ Witness ❑ Notary Public (name of business: _____)

Name: _____ Phone: _____

Address: _____

Document(s) to which they are acting: _____

_____

Type (select one): ❑ Witness ❑ Notary Public (name of business: _____)

Name: _____ Phone: _____

Address: _____

Document(s) to which they are acting: _____

_____

Type (select one): ❑ Witness ❑ Notary Public (name of business: _____)

Name: _____ Phone: _____

Address: _____

Document(s) to which they are acting: _____

_____

Type (select one): ❑ Witness ❑ Notary Public (name of business: _____)

Name: _____ Phone: _____

Address: _____

Document(s) to which they are acting: _____

_____

Type (select one): ❑ Witness ❑ Notary Public (name of business: _____)

Name: _____ Phone: _____

Address: _____

Document(s) to which they are acting: _____

_____

Type (select one): ❑ Witness ❑ Notary Public (name of business: _____)

Name: _____ Phone: _____

Address: _____

Document(s) to which they are acting: _____

_____

G. Executor

Type (select one): ❑ Executor ❑ Alternate executor

Name: _____ Phone: _____

Address: _____

Shared responsibility: ❑ No ❑ Yes, with name: _____

    Address: _____

    Phone: _____

Type (select one): ❑ Executor ❑ Alternate executor

Name: _____ Phone: _____

Address: _____

Shared responsibility: ❑ No ❑ Yes, with name: _____

    Address: _____

    Phone: _____

Type (select one): ❑ Executor ❑ Alternate executor

Name: _____ Phone: _____

Address: _____

Shared responsibility: ❑ No ❑ Yes, with name: _____

    Address: _____

    Phone: _____

Type (select one): ❑ Executor ❑ Alternate executor

Name: _____ Phone: _____

Address: _____

Shared responsibility: ❑ No ❑ Yes, with name: _____

    Address: _____

    Phone: _____

Type (select one): ❑ Executor ❑ Alternate executor

Name: _____ Phone: _____

Address: _____

Shared responsibility: ❑ No ❑ Yes, with name: _____

    Address: _____

    Phone: _____

Type (select one): ❑ Executor ❑ Alternate executor

Name: _____ Phone: _____

Address: _____

Shared responsibility: ❑ No ❑ Yes, with name: _____

    Address: _____

    Phone: _____

Type (select one): ❏ Executor ❏ Alternate executor

Name: _____ Phone: _____

Address: _____

Shared responsibility: ❏ No ❏ Yes, with name: _____

    Address: _____

    Phone: _____

Type (select one): ❏ Executor ❏ Alternate executor

Name: _____ Phone: _____

Address: _____

Shared responsibility: ❏ No ❏ Yes, with name: _____

    Address: _____

    Phone: _____

Type (select one): ❏ Executor ❏ Alternate executor

Name: _____ Phone: _____

Address: _____

Shared responsibility: ❏ No ❏ Yes, with name: _____

    Address: _____

    Phone: _____

H. Trustees

Type (select one): ❏ Trustee ❏ Alternate Trustee

Name: _____ Phone: _____

Address: _____

Compensation: $_____ Duration: _____

Documents located: _____

Shared responsibility: ❏ No ❏ Yes, with name: _____

    Address: _____

    Phone: _____

Description of property in trust: _____

_____

_____

_____

_____

Instructions: _____

_____

_____

_____

Type (select one): ☐ Trustee ☐ Alternate Trustee

Name: _____ Phone: _____

Address: _____

Compensation: $_____ Duration: _____

Documents located: _____

Shared responsibility: ☐ No ☐ Yes, with name: _____

    Address: _____

    Phone: _____

Description of property in trust: _____

_____

_____

_____

_____

Instructions: _____

_____

_____

_____

Type (select one): ❑ Trustee ❑ Alternate Trustee

Name: _____ Phone: _____

Address: _____

Compensation: $_____ Duration: _____

Documents located: _____

Shared responsibility: ❑ No ❑ Yes, with name: _____

    Address: _____

    Phone: _____

Description of property in trust: _____

_____

_____

_____

_____

Instructions: _____

_____

_____

_____

Type (select one): ❏ Trustee ❏ Alternate Trustee

Name: _____ Phone: _____

Address: _____

Compensation: $_____ Duration: _____

Documents located: _____

Shared responsibility: ❏ No ❏ Yes, with name: _____

    Address: _____

    Phone: _____

Description of property in trust: _____

_____

_____

_____

_____

Instructions: _____

_____

_____

_____

Type (select one): ❏ Trustee ❏ Alternate Trustee

Name: _____ Phone: _____

Address: _____

Compensation: $_____ Duration: _____

Documents located: _____

Shared responsibility: ❏ No ❏ Yes, with name: _____

    Address: _____

    Phone: _____

Description of property in trust: _____

_____

_____

_____

_____

Instructions: _____

_____

_____

_____

Type (select one): ❑ Trustee ❑ Alternate Trustee

Name: _____ Phone: _____

Address: _____

Compensation: $_____ Duration: _____

Documents located: _____

Shared responsibility: ❑ No ❑ Yes, with name: _____

    Address: _____

    Phone: _____

Description of property in trust: _____

_____

_____

_____

_____

Instructions: _____

_____

_____

_____

2. Property

A. Real Estate

Type (select one): ❑ Homestead ❑ Other residence ❑ Commercial ❑ Other: _____

Address: _____

Name/description of property: _____

Location of documents/title: _____

Property given by (select one): ❑ Will ❑ Trust ❑ Gift ❑ Other: _____

Payoff all debts before distributing: ❑ No ❑ Yes, pay from: _____

Primary Beneficiary: _____ Phone: _____

    Address: _____

    Shared: ❑ No ❑ Yes, percentage given: _____% shared with_____

    _____

Alternate Primary Beneficiary: _____ Phone: _____

    Address: _____

    Shared: ❑ No ❑ Yes, percentage given: _____% shared with_____

    _____

Mortgage: ❑ No ❑ Yes, origination date: _____ Amount: $_____

    Estimated pay-off date: _____ Monthly payments: $_____

    Account number: _____ Auto pay enabled: ❑ No ❑ Yes

    Mortgagor holder/bank's name: _____

    Agent's name: _____ Phone: _____

    Address: _____

    Online username: _____ Password: _____

Equity line: ❑ No ❑ Yes, origination date: _____ Amount: $_____

    Estimated pay-off date: _____ Monthly payments: $_____

    Account number: _____ Auto pay enabled: ❑ No ❑ Yes

    Equity holder/bank's name: _____

    Agent's name: _____ Phone: _____

    Address: _____

    Online username: _____ Password: _____

Property manager: ❑ No ❑ Yes, name: _____ Phone: _____

    Address: _____

Insurance policy: ❑ No ❑ Yes (see *Insurance and Annuities* section for more details)

    Brief description/details: _____

Type (select one): ❑ Homestead ❑ Other residence ❑ Commercial ❑ Other: _____

Address: _____

Name/description of property: _____

Location of documents/title: _____

Property given by (select one): ❑ Will ❑ Trust ❑ Gift ❑ Other: _____

Payoff all debts before distributing: ❑ No ❑ Yes, pay from: _____

Primary Beneficiary: _____ Phone: _____

    Address: _____

    Shared: ❑ No ❑ Yes, percentage given: _____% shared with_____

    _____

Alternate Primary Beneficiary: _____ Phone: _____

    Address: _____

    Shared: ❑ No ❑ Yes, percentage given: _____% shared with_____

    _____

Mortgage: ❑ No ❑ Yes, origination date: _____ Amount: $_____

    Estimated pay-off date: _____ Monthly payments: $_____

    Account number: _____ Auto pay enabled: ❑ No ❑ Yes

    Mortgagor holder/bank's name: _____

    Agent's name: _____ Phone: _____

    Address: _____

    Online username: _____ Password: _____

Equity line: ❑ No ❑ Yes, origination date: _____ Amount: $_____

    Estimated pay-off date: _____ Monthly payments: $_____

    Account number: _____ Auto pay enabled: ❑ No ❑ Yes

Equity holder/bank's name: _____

Agent's name: _____ Phone: _____

Address: _____

Online username: _____ Password: _____

Property manager: ❑ No ❑ Yes, name: _____ Phone: _____

Address: _____

Insurance policy: ❑ No ❑ Yes (see *Insurance and Annuities* section for more details)

Brief description/details: _____

Type (select one): ❑ Homestead ❑ Other residence ❑ Commercial ❑ Other: _____

Address: _____

Name/description of property: _____

Location of documents/title: _____

Property given by (select one): ❑ Will ❑ Trust ❑ Gift ❑ Other: _____

Payoff all debts before distributing: ❑ No ❑ Yes, pay from: _____

Primary Beneficiary: _____ Phone: _____

    Address: _____

    Shared: ❑ No ❑ Yes, percentage given: _____% shared with_____

    _____

Alternate Primary Beneficiary: _____ Phone: _____

    Address: _____

    Shared: ❑ No ❑ Yes, percentage given: _____% shared with_____

    _____

Mortgage: ❑ No ❑ Yes, origination date: _____ Amount: $_____

    Estimated pay-off date: _____ Monthly payments: $_____

    Account number: _____ Auto pay enabled: ❑ No ❑ Yes

    Mortgagor holder/bank's name: _____

    Agent's name: _____ Phone: _____

    Address: _____

    Online username: _____ Password: _____

Equity line: ❑ No ❑ Yes, origination date: _____ Amount: $_____

    Estimated pay-off date: _____ Monthly payments: $_____

    Account number: _____ Auto pay enabled: ❑ No ❑ Yes

Equity holder/bank's name: _____

Agent's name: _____ Phone: _____

Address: _____

Online username: _____ Password: _____

Property manager: ☐ No ☐ Yes, name: _____ Phone: _____

Address: _____

Insurance policy: ☐ No ☐ Yes (see *Insurance and Annuities* section for more details)

Brief description/details: _____

B. Bank Accounts

Bank name: _____ Account number: _____

Contact name: _____ Phone: _____

Branch address: _____

Location of documents: _____

Online username: _____ Password: _____

Savings account: ❑ No ❑ Yes, account number: _____

　　　Joint account: ❑ No ❑ Yes, with: _____

Checking account: ❑ No ❑ Yes, account number: _____

　　　Joint account: ❑ No ❑ Yes, with: _____

　　　Checkbook: ❑ No ❑ Yes, location of checkbook: _____

Debit card: ❑ No ❑ Yes, number: _____ Expires: _____

　　　❑ Visa ❑ MasterCard　　　❑ Other card holders: _____

Direct deposit: ❑ No ❑ Yes, amount: $_____Frequency: ❑ Monthly ❑ Bi-Weekly
　　　❑ Weekly ❑ Annual ❑ Other: _____

　　　Payment received from (name): _____

　　　Contact name: _____ Phone: _____

　　　Address: _____

Auto pay: ❑ No ❑ Yes, to/date(s) drafted: _____

_____

_____

Safety deposit box: ❑ No ❑ Yes, key location: _____ Code: _____

　　　Names on account: _____ Payment methods: _____

　　　Payment on Death set-up: ❑ No ❑ Yes, beneficiary: _____

Bank name: _____ Account number: _____

Contact name: _____ Phone: _____

Branch address: _____

Location of documents: _____

Online username: _____ Password: _____

Savings account: ❑ No ❑ Yes, account number: _____

  Joint account: ❑ No ❑ Yes, with: _____

Checking account: ❑ No ❑ Yes, account number: _____

  Joint account: ❑ No ❑ Yes, with: _____

  Checkbook: ❑ No ❑ Yes, location of checkbook: _____

Debit card: ❑ No ❑ Yes, number: _____ Expires: _____

  ❑ Visa ❑ MasterCard ❑ Other card holders: _____

Direct deposit: ❑ No ❑ Yes, amount: $_____Frequency: ❑ Monthly ❑ Bi-Weekly
❑ Weekly ❑ Annual ❑ Other: _____

  Payment received from (name): _____

  Contact name: _____ Phone: _____

  Address: _____

Auto pay: ❑ No ❑ Yes, to/date(s) drafted: _____

_____

_____

Safety deposit box: ❑ No ❑ Yes, key location: _____ Code: _____

  Names on account: _____ Payment methods: _____

  Payment on Death set-up: ❑ No ❑ Yes, beneficiary: _____

Bank name: _____ Account number: _____

Contact name: _____ Phone: _____

Branch address: _____

Location of documents: _____

Online username: _____ Password: _____

Savings account: ❑ No ❑ Yes, account number: _____

    Joint account: ❑ No ❑ Yes, with: _____

Checking account: ❑ No ❑ Yes, account number: _____

    Joint account: ❑ No ❑ Yes, with: _____

    Checkbook: ❑ No ❑ Yes, location of checkbook: _____

Debit card: ❑ No ❑ Yes, number: _____ Expires: _____

    ❑ Visa ❑ MasterCard   ❑ Other card holders: _____

Direct deposit: ❑ No ❑ Yes, amount: $_____ Frequency: ❑ Monthly ❑ Bi-Weekly
❑ Weekly ❑ Annual ❑ Other: _____

    Payment received from (name): _____

    Contact name: _____ Phone: _____

    Address: _____

Auto pay: ❑ No ❑ Yes, to/date(s) drafted: _____

_____

_____

Safety deposit box: ❑ No ❑ Yes, key location: _____ Code: _____

    Names on account: _____ Payment methods: _____

    Payment on Death set-up: ❑ No ❑ Yes, beneficiary: _____

Bank name: _____ Account number: _____

Contact name: _____ Phone: _____

Branch address: _____

Location of documents: _____

Online username: _____ Password: _____

Savings account: ❑ No ❑ Yes, account number: _____

    Joint account: ❑ No ❑ Yes, with: _____

Checking account: ❑ No ❑ Yes, account number: _____

    Joint account: ❑ No ❑ Yes, with: _____

    Checkbook: ❑ No ❑ Yes, location of checkbook: _____

Debit card: ❑ No ❑ Yes, number: _____ Expires: _____

    ❑ Visa ❑ MasterCard   ❑ Other card holders: _____

Direct deposit: ❑ No ❑ Yes, amount: $_____ Frequency: ❑ Monthly ❑ Bi-Weekly
❑ Weekly ❑ Annual ❑ Other: _____

    Payment received from (name): _____

    Contact name: _____ Phone: _____

    Address: _____

Auto pay: ❑ No ❑ Yes, to/date(s) drafted: _____

_____

_____

Safety deposit box: ❑ No ❑ Yes, key location: _____ Code: _____

    Names on account: _____ Payment methods: _____

    Payment on Death set-up: ❑ No ❑ Yes, beneficiary: _____

Bank name: _____ Account number: _____

Contact name: _____ Phone: _____

Branch address: _____

Location of documents: _____

Online username: _____ Password: _____

Savings account: ❏ No ❏ Yes, account number: _____

    Joint account: ❏ No ❏ Yes, with: _____

Checking account: ❏ No ❏ Yes, account number: _____

    Joint account: ❏ No ❏ Yes, with: _____

    Checkbook: ❏ No ❏ Yes, location of checkbook: _____

Debit card: ❏ No ❏ Yes, number: _____ Expires: _____

    ❏ Visa ❏ MasterCard   ❏ Other card holders: _____

Direct deposit: ❏ No ❏ Yes, amount: $_____ Frequency: ❏ Monthly ❏ Bi-Weekly
    ❏ Weekly ❏ Annual ❏ Other: _____

    Payment received from (name): _____

    Contact name: _____ Phone: _____

    Address: _____

Auto pay: ❏ No ❏ Yes, to/date(s) drafted: _____

_____

_____

Safety deposit box: ❏ No ❏ Yes, key location: _____ Code: _____

    Names on account: _____ Payment methods: _____

    Payment on Death set-up: ❏ No ❏ Yes, beneficiary: _____

C.   Insurance and Annuities

Type : ❏ Life ❏ Worker's compensation ❏ Health ❏ Medicare ❏ Medicaid ❏ Dental ❏ Vision
❏ Disability ❏ Long-term care ❏ Auto ❏ Home ❏ Renter's ❏ Military ❏ Annuity
❏ Other: _____

Coverage description: _____

_____

Location of documents: _____

Policy number: _____ Date issued: _____

Online username: _____ Password: _____

Status: ❏ Active ❏ Expired ❏ Discharged, reason: _____

Company/provider name: _____

Agent name: _____ Phone: _____

Branch address: _____

Part of employment: ❏ No ❏ Yes, employer name: _____

Current employer: ❏ No (Reason for discharge: _____) ❏ Yes

Contact name: _____ Phone: _____

Address: _____

Dates of employment: _____ to _____

Type : ❑ Life ❑ Worker's compensation ❑ Health ❑ Medicare ❑ Medicaid ❑ Dental ❑ Vision ❑ Disability ❑ Long-term care ❑ Auto ❑ Home ❑ Renter's ❑ Military ❑ Annuity ❑ Other: _____

Coverage description: _____

_____

Location of documents: _____

Policy number: _____ Date issued: _____

Online username: _____ Password: _____

Status: ❑ Active ❑ Expired ❑ Discharged, reason: _____

Company/provider name: _____

Agent name: _____ Phone: _____

Branch address: _____

Part of employment: ❑ No ❑ Yes, employer name: _____

Current employer: ❑ No (Reason for discharge: _____) ❑ Yes

Contact name: _____ Phone: _____

Address: _____

Dates of employment: _____ to _____

Type : ❑ Life ❑ Worker's compensation ❑ Health ❑ Medicare ❑ Medicaid ❑ Dental ❑ Vision ❑ Disability ❑ Long-term care ❑ Auto ❑ Home ❑ Renter's ❑ Military ❑ Annuity ❑ Other: _____

Coverage description: _____

_____

Location of documents: _____

Policy number: _____ Date issued: _____

Online username: _____ Password: _____

Status: ❑ Active ❑ Expired ❑ Discharged, reason: _____

Company/provider name: _____

    Agent name: _____ Phone: _____

    Branch address: _____

Part of employment: ❑ No ❑ Yes, employer name: _____

    Current employer: ❑ No (Reason for discharge: _____) ❑ Yes

    Contact name: _____ Phone: _____

    Address: _____

    Dates of employment: _____ to _____

Type : ❑ Life ❑ Worker's compensation ❑ Health ❑ Medicare ❑ Medicaid ❑ Dental ❑ Vision ❑ Disability ❑ Long-term care ❑ Auto ❑ Home ❑ Renter's ❑ Military ❑ Annuity ❑ Other: _____

Coverage description: _____

_____

Location of documents: _____

Policy number: _____ Date issued: _____

Online username: _____ Password: _____

Status: ❑ Active ❑ Expired ❑ Discharged, reason: _____

Company/provider name: _____

 Agent name: _____ Phone: _____

 Branch address: _____

Part of employment: ❑ No ❑ Yes, employer name: _____

 Current employer: ❑ No (Reason for discharge: _____) ❑ Yes

 Contact name: _____ Phone: _____

 Address: _____

 Dates of employment: _____ to _____

Type : ❏ Life ❏ Worker's compensation ❏ Health ❏ Medicare ❏ Medicaid ❏ Dental ❏ Vision ❏ Disability ❏ Long-term care ❏ Auto ❏ Home ❏ Renter's ❏ Military ❏ Annuity ❏ Other: _____

Coverage description: _____

_____

Location of documents: _____

Policy number: _____ Date issued: _____

Online username: _____ Password: _____

Status: ❏ Active ❏ Expired ❏ Discharged, reason: _____

Company/provider name: _____

   Agent name: _____ Phone: _____

   Branch address: _____

Part of employment: ❏ No ❏ Yes, employer name: _____

   Current employer: ❏ No (Reason for discharge: _____) ❏ Yes

   Contact name: _____ Phone: _____

   Address: _____

   Dates of employment: _____ to _____

Type : ❏ Life ❏ Worker's compensation ❏ Health ❏ Medicare ❏ Medicaid ❏ Dental ❏ Vision
❏ Disability ❏ Long-term care ❏ Auto ❏ Home ❏ Renter's ❏ Military ❏ Annuity
❏ Other: _____

Coverage description: _____

_____

Location of documents: _____

Policy number: _____ Date issued: _____

Online username: _____ Password: _____

Status: ❏ Active ❏ Expired ❏ Discharged, reason: _____

Company/provider name: _____

    Agent name: _____ Phone: _____

    Branch address: _____

Part of employment: ❏ No ❏ Yes, employer name: _____

    Current employer: ❏ No (Reason for discharge: _____) ❏ Yes

    Contact name: _____ Phone: _____

    Address: _____

    Dates of employment: _____ to _____

Type : ❑ Life ❑ Worker's compensation ❑ Health ❑ Medicare ❑ Medicaid ❑ Dental ❑ Vision ❑ Disability ❑ Long-term care ❑ Auto ❑ Home ❑ Renter's ❑ Military ❑ Annuity ❑ Other: _____

Coverage description: _____

_____

Location of documents: _____

Policy number: _____ Date issued: _____

Online username: _____ Password: _____

Status: ❑ Active ❑ Expired ❑ Discharged, reason: _____

Company/provider name: _____

    Agent name: _____ Phone: _____

    Branch address: _____

Part of employment: ❑ No ❑ Yes, employer name: _____

    Current employer: ❑ No (Reason for discharge: _____) ❑ Yes

    Contact name: _____ Phone: _____

    Address: _____

    Dates of employment: _____ to _____

Type : ❑ Life ❑ Worker's compensation ❑ Health ❑ Medicare ❑ Medicaid ❑ Dental ❑ Vision ❑ Disability ❑ Long-term care ❑ Auto ❑ Home ❑ Renter's ❑ Military ❑ Annuity ❑ Other: _____

Coverage description: _____

_____

Location of documents: _____

Policy number: _____ Date issued: _____

Online username: _____ Password: _____

Status: ❑ Active ❑ Expired ❑ Discharged, reason: _____

Company/provider name: _____

    Agent name: _____ Phone: _____

    Branch address: _____

Part of employment: ❑ No ❑ Yes, employer name: _____

    Current employer: ❑ No (Reason for discharge: _____) ❑ Yes

    Contact name: _____ Phone: _____

    Address: _____

    Dates of employment: _____ to _____

Type : ❑ Life ❑ Worker's compensation ❑ Health ❑ Medicare ❑ Medicaid ❑ Dental ❑ Vision ❑ Disability ❑ Long-term care ❑ Auto ❑ Home ❑ Renter's ❑ Military ❑ Annuity ❑ Other: _____

Coverage description: _____

_____

Location of documents: _____

Policy number: _____ Date issued: _____

Online username: _____ Password: _____

Status: ❑ Active ❑ Expired ❑ Discharged, reason: _____

Company/provider name: _____

Agent name: _____ Phone: _____

Branch address: _____

Part of employment: ❑ No ❑ Yes, employer name: _____

Current employer: ❑ No (Reason for discharge: _____) ❑ Yes

Contact name: _____ Phone: _____

Address: _____

Dates of employment: _____ to _____

Type : ❑ Life ❑ Worker's compensation ❑ Health ❑ Medicare ❑ Medicaid ❑ Dental ❑ Vision ❑ Disability ❑ Long-term care ❑ Auto ❑ Home ❑ Renter's ❑ Military ❑ Annuity ❑ Other: _____

Coverage description: _____

_____

Location of documents: _____

Policy number: _____ Date issued: _____

Online username: _____ Password: _____

Status: ❑ Active ❑ Expired ❑ Discharged, reason: _____

Company/provider name: _____

    Agent name: _____ Phone: _____

    Branch address: _____

Part of employment: ❑ No ❑ Yes, employer name: _____

    Current employer: ❑ No (Reason for discharge: _____) ❑ Yes

    Contact name: _____ Phone: _____

    Address: _____

    Dates of employment: _____ to _____

Type : ❑ Life ❑ Worker's compensation ❑ Health ❑ Medicare ❑ Medicaid ❑ Dental ❑ Vision ❑ Disability ❑ Long-term care ❑ Auto ❑ Home ❑ Renter's ❑ Military ❑ Annuity ❑ Other: _____

Coverage description: _____

_____

Location of documents: _____

Policy number: _____ Date issued: _____

Online username: _____ Password: _____

Status: ❑ Active ❑ Expired ❑ Discharged, reason: _____

Company/provider name: _____

    Agent name: _____ Phone: _____

    Branch address: _____

Part of employment: ❑ No ❑ Yes, employer name: _____

    Current employer: ❑ No (Reason for discharge: _____) ❑ Yes

    Contact name: _____ Phone: _____

    Address: _____

    Dates of employment: _____ to _____

Type : ❑ Life ❑ Worker's compensation ❑ Health ❑ Medicare ❑ Medicaid ❑ Dental ❑ Vision ❑ Disability ❑ Long-term care ❑ Auto ❑ Home ❑ Renter's ❑ Military ❑ Annuity ❑ Other: _____

Coverage description: _____

_____

Location of documents: _____

Policy number: _____ Date issued: _____

Online username: _____ Password: _____

Status: ❑ Active ❑ Expired ❑ Discharged, reason: _____

Company/provider name: _____

    Agent name: _____ Phone: _____

    Branch address: _____

Part of employment: ❑ No ❑ Yes, employer name: _____

    Current employer: ❑ No (Reason for discharge: _____) ❑ Yes

    Contact name: _____ Phone: _____

    Address: _____

    Dates of employment: _____ to _____

Type : ❑ Life ❑ Worker's compensation ❑ Health ❑ Medicare ❑ Medicaid ❑ Dental ❑ Vision
❑ Disability ❑ Long-term care ❑ Auto ❑ Home ❑ Renter's ❑ Military ❑ Annuity
❑ Other: _____

Coverage description: _____

_____

Location of documents: _____

Policy number: _____ Date issued: _____

Online username: _____ Password: _____

Status: ❑ Active ❑ Expired ❑ Discharged, reason: _____

Company/provider name: _____

    Agent name: _____ Phone: _____

    Branch address: _____

Part of employment: ❑ No ❑ Yes, employer name: _____

    Current employer: ❑ No (Reason for discharge: _____) ❑ Yes

    Contact name: _____ Phone: _____

    Address: _____

    Dates of employment: _____ to _____

Type : ❑ Life ❑ Worker's compensation ❑ Health ❑ Medicare ❑ Medicaid ❑ Dental ❑ Vision ❑ Disability ❑ Long-term care ❑ Auto ❑ Home ❑ Renter's ❑ Military ❑ Annuity ❑ Other: _____

Coverage description: _____

_____

Location of documents: _____

Policy number: _____ Date issued: _____

Online username: _____ Password: _____

Status: ❑ Active ❑ Expired ❑ Discharged, reason: _____

Company/provider name: _____

Agent name: _____ Phone: _____

Branch address: _____

Part of employment: ❑ No ❑ Yes, employer name: _____

Current employer: ❑ No (Reason for discharge: _____) ❑ Yes

Contact name: _____ Phone: _____

Address: _____

Dates of employment: _____ to _____

Type : ❑ Life ❑ Worker's compensation ❑ Health ❑ Medicare ❑ Medicaid ❑ Dental ❑ Vision ❑ Disability ❑ Long-term care ❑ Auto ❑ Home ❑ Renter's ❑ Military ❑ Annuity ❑ Other: _____

Coverage description: _____

_____

Location of documents: _____

Policy number: _____ Date issued: _____

Online username: _____ Password: _____

Status: ❑ Active ❑ Expired ❑ Discharged, reason: _____

Company/provider name: _____

    Agent name: _____ Phone: _____

    Branch address: _____

Part of employment: ❑ No ❑ Yes, employer name: _____

    Current employer: ❑ No (Reason for discharge: _____) ❑ Yes

    Contact name: _____ Phone: _____

    Address: _____

    Dates of employment: _____ to _____

Type : ❑ Life ❑ Worker's compensation ❑ Health ❑ Medicare ❑ Medicaid ❑ Dental ❑ Vision ❑ Disability ❑ Long-term care ❑ Auto ❑ Home ❑ Renter's ❑ Military ❑ Annuity ❑ Other: _____

Coverage description: _____

_____

Location of documents: _____

Policy number: _____ Date issued: _____

Online username: _____ Password: _____

Status: ❑ Active ❑ Expired ❑ Discharged, reason: _____

Company/provider name: _____

    Agent name: _____ Phone: _____

    Branch address: _____

Part of employment: ❑ No ❑ Yes, employer name: _____

    Current employer: ❑ No (Reason for discharge: _____) ❑ Yes

    Contact name: _____ Phone: _____

    Address: _____

    Dates of employment: _____ to _____

Type : ❑ Life ❑ Worker's compensation ❑ Health ❑ Medicare ❑ Medicaid ❑ Dental ❑ Vision ❑ Disability ❑ Long-term care ❑ Auto ❑ Home ❑ Renter's ❑ Military ❑ Annuity ❑ Other: _____

Coverage description: _____

_____

Location of documents: _____

Policy number: _____ Date issued: _____

Online username: _____ Password: _____

Status: ❑ Active ❑ Expired ❑ Discharged, reason: _____

Company/provider name: _____

    Agent name: _____ Phone: _____

    Branch address: _____

Part of employment: ❑ No ❑ Yes, employer name: _____

    Current employer: ❑ No (Reason for discharge: _____) ❑ Yes

    Contact name: _____ Phone: _____

    Address: _____

    Dates of employment: _____ to _____

Type : ❑ Life ❑ Worker's compensation ❑ Health ❑ Medicare ❑ Medicaid ❑ Dental ❑ Vision ❑ Disability ❑ Long-term care ❑ Auto ❑ Home ❑ Renter's ❑ Military ❑ Annuity ❑ Other: _____

Coverage description: _____

_____

Location of documents: _____

Policy number: _____ Date issued: _____

Online username: _____ Password: _____

Status: ❑ Active ❑ Expired ❑ Discharged, reason: _____

Company/provider name: _____

    Agent name: _____ Phone: _____

    Branch address: _____

Part of employment: ❑ No ❑ Yes, employer name: _____

    Current employer: ❑ No (Reason for discharge: _____) ❑ Yes

    Contact name: _____ Phone: _____

    Address: _____

    Dates of employment: _____ to _____

Type : ❑ Life ❑ Worker's compensation ❑ Health ❑ Medicare ❑ Medicaid ❑ Dental ❑ Vision ❑ Disability ❑ Long-term care ❑ Auto ❑ Home ❑ Renter's ❑ Military ❑ Annuity ❑ Other: _____

Coverage description: _____

_____

Location of documents: _____

Policy number: _____ Date issued: _____

Online username: _____ Password: _____

Status: ❑ Active ❑ Expired ❑ Discharged, reason: _____

Company/provider name: _____

    Agent name: _____ Phone: _____

    Branch address: _____

Part of employment: ❑ No ❑ Yes, employer name: _____

    Current employer: ❑ No (Reason for discharge: _____) ❑ Yes

    Contact name: _____ Phone: _____

    Address: _____

    Dates of employment: _____ to _____

Type : ❑ Life ❑ Worker's compensation ❑ Health ❑ Medicare ❑ Medicaid ❑ Dental ❑ Vision ❑ Disability ❑ Long-term care ❑ Auto ❑ Home ❑ Renter's ❑ Military ❑ Annuity ❑ Other: _____

Coverage description: _____

_____

Location of documents: _____

Policy number: _____ Date issued: _____

Online username: _____ Password: _____

Status: ❑ Active ❑ Expired ❑ Discharged, reason: _____

Company/provider name: _____

    Agent name: _____ Phone: _____

    Branch address: _____

Part of employment: ❑ No ❑ Yes, employer name: _____

    Current employer: ❑ No (Reason for discharge: _____) ❑ Yes

    Contact name: _____ Phone: _____

    Address: _____

    Dates of employment: _____ to _____

Type : ❑ Life ❑ Worker's compensation ❑ Health ❑ Medicare ❑ Medicaid ❑ Dental ❑ Vision ❑ Disability ❑ Long-term care ❑ Auto ❑ Home ❑ Renter's ❑ Military ❑ Annuity ❑ Other: _____

Coverage description: _____

_____

Location of documents: _____

Policy number: _____ Date issued: _____

Online username: _____ Password: _____

Status: ❑ Active ❑ Expired ❑ Discharged, reason: _____

Company/provider name: _____

    Agent name: _____ Phone: _____

    Branch address: _____

Part of employment: ❑ No ❑ Yes, employer name: _____

    Current employer: ❑ No (Reason for discharge: _____) ❑ Yes

    Contact name: _____ Phone: _____

    Address: _____

    Dates of employment: _____ to _____

D. Death Benefits

Status (select one): ❑ Current ❑ Past ❑ Spouse ❑ Other: _____

Policy type (select one): ❑ Group life insurance ❑ Group health insurance (death benefits)
❑ COBRA ❑ Deferred compensation ❑ Credit union deposits ❑ Pension (survivors' benefits)
❑ Profit-sharing (survivors' benefits) ❑ Unpaid salary ❑ Other: _____

Coverage description: _____

_____

Location of documents: _____

Policy number: _____ Date issued: _____

Online username: _____ Password: _____

Status: ❑ Active ❑ Expired ❑ Discharged, reason: _____

Company/provider name: _____

    Agent name: _____ Phone: _____

    Branch address: _____

Part of employment: ❑ No ❑ Yes, employer name: _____

    Current employer: ❑ No (Reason for discharge: _____) ❑ Yes

    Contact name: _____ Phone: _____

    Address: _____

    Dates of employment: _____ to _____

If killed on the job, additional benefits may be paid to the family: ❑ No ❑ Yes, from: ❑ Worker's
compensation ❑ Accidental travel insurance, common carrier insurance, tickets purchased
by credit card ❑ Other: _____

Status (select one): ❑ Current ❑ Past ❑ Spouse ❑ Other: _____

Policy type (select one): ❑ Group life insurance ❑ Group health insurance (death benefits)
❑ COBRA ❑ Deferred compensation ❑ Credit union deposits ❑ Pension (survivors' benefits)
❑ Profit-sharing (survivors' benefits) ❑ Unpaid salary ❑ Other: _____

Coverage description: _____

_____

Location of documents: _____

Policy number: _____ Date issued: _____

Online username: _____ Password: _____

Status: ❑ Active ❑ Expired ❑ Discharged, reason: _____

Company/provider name: _____

    Agent name: _____ Phone: _____

    Branch address: _____

Part of employment: ❑ No ❑ Yes, employer name: _____

    Current employer: ❑ No (Reason for discharge: _____) ❑ Yes

    Contact name: _____ Phone: _____

    Address: _____

    Dates of employment: _____ to _____

If killed on the job, additional benefits may be paid to the family: ❑ No ❑ Yes, from: ❑ Worker's
compensation ❑ Accidental travel insurance, common carrier insurance, tickets purchased
by credit card ❑ Other: _____

Status (select one): ❏ Current ❏ Past ❏ Spouse ❏ Other: _____

Policy type (select one): ❏ Group life insurance ❏ Group health insurance (death benefits)
❏ COBRA ❏ Deferred compensation ❏ Credit union deposits ❏ Pension (survivors' benefits)
❏ Profit-sharing (survivors' benefits) ❏ Unpaid salary ❏ Other: _____

Coverage description: _____

_____

Location of documents: _____

Policy number: _____ Date issued: _____

Online username: _____ Password: _____

Status: ❏ Active ❏ Expired ❏ Discharged, reason: _____

Company/provider name: _____

    Agent name: _____ Phone: _____

    Branch address: _____

Part of employment: ❏ No ❏ Yes, employer name: _____

    Current employer: ❏ No (Reason for discharge: _____) ❏ Yes

    Contact name: _____ Phone: _____

    Address: _____

    Dates of employment: _____ to _____

If killed on the job, additional benefits may be paid to the family: ❏ No ❏ Yes, from: ❏ Worker's
    compensation ❏ Accidental travel insurance, common carrier insurance, tickets purchased
    by credit card ❏ Other: _____

Status (select one): ❏ Current ❏ Past ❏ Spouse ❏ Other: _____

Policy type (select one): ❏ Group life insurance ❏ Group health insurance (death benefits)
❏ COBRA ❏ Deferred compensation ❏ Credit union deposits ❏ Pension (survivors' benefits)
❏ Profit-sharing (survivors' benefits) ❏ Unpaid salary ❏ Other: _____

Coverage description: _____

_____

Location of documents: _____

Policy number: _____ Date issued: _____

Online username: _____ Password: _____

Status: ❏ Active ❏ Expired ❏ Discharged, reason: _____

Company/provider name: _____

    Agent name: _____ Phone: _____

    Branch address: _____

Part of employment: ❏ No ❏ Yes, employer name: _____

    Current employer: ❏ No (Reason for discharge: _____) ❏ Yes

    Contact name: _____ Phone: _____

    Address: _____

    Dates of employment: _____ to _____

If killed on the job, additional benefits may be paid to the family: ❏ No ❏ Yes, from: ❏ Worker's
    compensation ❏ Accidental travel insurance, common carrier insurance, tickets purchased
    by credit card ❏ Other: _____

Status (select one): ❑ Current ❑ Past ❑ Spouse ❑ Other: _____

Policy type (select one): ❑ Group life insurance ❑ Group health insurance (death benefits)
❑ COBRA ❑ Deferred compensation ❑ Credit union deposits ❑ Pension (survivors' benefits)
❑ Profit-sharing (survivors' benefits) ❑ Unpaid salary ❑ Other: _____

Coverage description: _____

_____

Location of documents: _____

Policy number: _____ Date issued: _____

Online username: _____ Password: _____

Status: ❑ Active ❑ Expired ❑ Discharged, reason: _____

Company/provider name: _____

    Agent name: _____ Phone: _____

    Branch address: _____

Part of employment: ❑ No ❑ Yes, employer name: _____

    Current employer: ❑ No (Reason for discharge: _____) ❑ Yes

    Contact name: _____ Phone: _____

    Address: _____

    Dates of employment: _____ to _____

If killed on the job, additional benefits may be paid to the family: ❑ No ❑ Yes, from: ❑ Worker's
    compensation ❑ Accidental travel insurance, common carrier insurance, tickets purchased
    by credit card ❑ Other: _____

Status (select one): ❑ Current ❑ Past ❑ Spouse ❑ Other: _____

Policy type (select one): ❑ Group life insurance ❑ Group health insurance (death benefits)
❑ COBRA ❑ Deferred compensation ❑ Credit union deposits ❑ Pension (survivors' benefits)
❑ Profit-sharing (survivors' benefits) ❑ Unpaid salary ❑ Other: _____

Coverage description: _____

_____

Location of documents: _____

Policy number: _____ Date issued: _____

Online username: _____ Password: _____

Status: ❑ Active ❑ Expired ❑ Discharged, reason: _____

Company/provider name: _____

    Agent name: _____ Phone: _____

    Branch address: _____

Part of employment: ❑ No ❑ Yes, employer name: _____

    Current employer: ❑ No (Reason for discharge: _____) ❑ Yes

    Contact name: _____ Phone: _____

    Address: _____

    Dates of employment: _____ to _____

If killed on the job, additional benefits may be paid to the family: ❑ No ❑ Yes, from: ❑ Worker's
    compensation ❑ Accidental travel insurance, common carrier insurance, tickets purchased
    by credit card ❑ Other: _____

Status (select one): ❑ Current ❑ Past ❑ Spouse ❑ Other: _____

Policy type (select one): ❑ Group life insurance ❑ Group health insurance (death benefits)
❑ COBRA ❑ Deferred compensation ❑ Credit union deposits ❑ Pension (survivors' benefits)
❑ Profit-sharing (survivors' benefits) ❑ Unpaid salary ❑ Other: _____

Coverage description: _____

_____

Location of documents: _____

Policy number: _____ Date issued: _____

Online username: _____ Password: _____

Status: ❑ Active ❑ Expired ❑ Discharged, reason: _____

Company/provider name: _____

    Agent name: _____ Phone: _____

    Branch address: _____

Part of employment: ❑ No ❑ Yes, employer name: _____

    Current employer: ❑ No (Reason for discharge: _____) ❑ Yes

    Contact name: _____ Phone: _____

    Address: _____

    Dates of employment: _____ to _____

If killed on the job, additional benefits may be paid to the family: ❑ No ❑ Yes, from: ❑ Worker's
    compensation ❑ Accidental travel insurance, common carrier insurance, tickets purchased
    by credit card ❑ Other: _____

E. Trusts

Trust title: _____

Beneficiary: _____ Phone: _____

    Address: _____

Child's trust: ❑ No ❑ Yes, DOB: _____ SSN: _____

    Relation: _____

    Personal guardian(s) ❑ No ❑ Yes, name(s): _____

        Address: _____

        Phone: _____

Location of documents: _____

Description of trust property: _____

_____

_____

Trust instructions: _____

Preparer's name: _____ Phone: _____

    Address: _____

    Company: _____ Date prepared: _____

Trustee name: _____ Phone: _____

    Address: _____

Alternate Trustee name: _____ Phone: _____

    Address: _____

Trust title: _____

Beneficiary: _____ Phone: _____

    Address: _____

Child's trust: ❑ No ❑ Yes, DOB: _____ SSN: _____

    Relation: _____

    Personal guardian(s) ❑ No ❑ Yes, name(s): _____

        Address: _____

        Phone: _____

Location of documents: _____

Description of trust property: _____

_____

_____

Trust instructions: _____

Preparer's name: _____ Phone: _____

    Address: _____

    Company: _____ Date prepared: _____

Trustee name: _____ Phone: _____

    Address: _____

Alternate Trustee name: _____ Phone: _____

    Address: _____

Trust title: _____

Beneficiary: _____ Phone: _____

    Address: _____

Child's trust: ☐ No ☐ Yes, DOB: _____ SSN: _____

    Relation: _____

    Personal guardian(s) ☐ No ☐ Yes, name(s): _____

        Address: _____

        Phone: _____

Location of documents: _____

Description of trust property: _____

_____

_____

Trust instructions: _____

Preparer's name: _____ Phone: _____

    Address: _____

    Company: _____ Date prepared: _____

Trustee name: _____ Phone: _____

    Address: _____

Alternate Trustee name: _____ Phone: _____

    Address: _____

Trust title: _____

Beneficiary: _____ Phone: _____

    Address: _____

Child's trust: ❑ No ❑ Yes, DOB: _____ SSN: _____

    Relation: _____

    Personal guardian(s) ❑ No ❑ Yes, name(s): _____

        Address: _____

        Phone: _____

Location of documents: _____

Description of trust property: _____

_____

_____

Trust instructions: _____

Preparer's name: _____ Phone: _____

    Address: _____

    Company: _____ Date prepared: _____

Trustee name: _____ Phone: _____

    Address: _____

Alternate Trustee name: _____ Phone: _____

    Address: _____

Trust title: _____

Beneficiary: _____ Phone: _____

    Address: _____

Child's trust: ❑ No ❑ Yes, DOB: _____ SSN: _____

    Relation: _____

    Personal guardian(s) ❑ No ❑ Yes, name(s): _____

        Address: _____

        Phone: _____

Location of documents: _____

Description of trust property: _____

_____

_____

Trust instructions: _____

Preparer's name: _____ Phone: _____

    Address: _____

    Company: _____ Date prepared: _____

Trustee name: _____ Phone: _____

    Address: _____

Alternate Trustee name: _____ Phone: _____

    Address: _____

Trust title: _____

Beneficiary: _____ Phone: _____

    Address: _____

Child's trust: ❑ No ❑ Yes, DOB: _____ SSN: _____

    Relation: _____

    Personal guardian(s) ❑ No ❑ Yes, name(s): _____

        Address: _____

        Phone: _____

Location of documents: _____

Description of trust property: _____

_____

_____

Trust instructions: _____

Preparer's name: _____ Phone: _____

    Address: _____

    Company: _____ Date prepared: _____

Trustee name: _____ Phone: _____

    Address: _____

Alternate Trustee name: _____ Phone: _____

    Address: _____

Trust title: _____

Beneficiary: _____ Phone: _____

    Address: _____

Child's trust: ❑ No ❑ Yes, DOB: _____ SSN: _____

    Relation: _____

    Personal guardian(s) ❑ No ❑ Yes, name(s): _____

        Address: _____

        Phone: _____

Location of documents: _____

Description of trust property: _____

    _____

    _____

Trust instructions: _____

Preparer's name: _____ Phone: _____

    Address: _____

    Company: _____ Date prepared: _____

Trustee name: _____ Phone: _____

    Address: _____

Alternate Trustee name: _____ Phone: _____

    Address: _____

F.   Non-Real Estate Debt

Debt (select one): ❑ Credit Card ❑ Student ❑ Auto ❑ Other: _____

Status: ❑ Active ❑ Grace ❑ Deferred ❑ Other: _____

Company/provider name: _____

    Contact name: _____ Phone: _____

    Address: _____

Location of documents: _____

Account number: _____ Auto pay: ❑ No ❑ Yes, amount: $ _____

Monthly due date: _____ Monthly payments: $_____

Origination date: _____ Original amount: $_____

Estimated pay-off date: _____

Online username: _____ Password: _____

Debt (select one): ❑ Credit Card ❑ Student ❑ Auto ❑ Other: _____

Status: ❑ Active ❑ Grace ❑ Deferred ❑ Other: _____

Company/provider name: _____

    Contact name: _____ Phone: _____

    Address: _____

Location of documents: _____

Account number: _____ Auto pay: ❑ No ❑ Yes, amount: $ _____

Monthly due date: _____ Monthly payments: $_____

Origination date: _____ Original amount: $_____

Estimated pay-off date: _____

Online username: _____ Password: _____

Debt (select one): ❏ Credit Card ❏ Student ❏ Auto ❏ Other: _____

Status: ❏ Active ❏ Grace ❏ Deferred ❏ Other: _____

Company/provider name: _____

     Contact name: _____ Phone: _____

     Address: _____

Location of documents: _____

Account number: _____ Auto pay: ❏ No ❏ Yes, amount: $ _____

Monthly due date: _____ Monthly payments: $_____

Origination date: _____ Original amount: $_____

Estimated pay-off date: _____

Online username: _____ Password: _____

Debt (select one): ❏ Credit Card ❏ Student ❏ Auto ❏ Other: _____

Status: ❏ Active ❏ Grace ❏ Deferred ❏ Other: _____

Company/provider name: _____

     Contact name: _____ Phone: _____

     Address: _____

Location of documents: _____

Account number: _____ Auto pay: ❏ No ❏ Yes, amount: $ _____

Monthly due date: _____ Monthly payments: $_____

Origination date: _____ Original amount: $_____

Estimated pay-off date: _____

Online username: _____ Password: _____

Debt (select one): ❑ Credit Card ❑ Student ❑ Auto ❑ Other: _____

Status: ❑ Active ❑ Grace ❑ Deferred ❑ Other: _____

Company/provider name: _____

    Contact name: _____ Phone: _____

    Address: _____

Location of documents: _____

Account number: _____ Auto pay: ❑ No ❑ Yes, amount: $ _____

Monthly due date: _____ Monthly payments: $_____

Origination date: _____ Original amount: $_____

Estimated pay-off date: _____

Online username: _____ Password: _____

Debt (select one): ❑ Credit Card ❑ Student ❑ Auto ❑ Other: _____

Status: ❑ Active ❑ Grace ❑ Deferred ❑ Other: _____

Company/provider name: _____

    Contact name: _____ Phone: _____

    Address: _____

Location of documents: _____

Account number: _____ Auto pay: ❑ No ❑ Yes, amount: $ _____

Monthly due date: _____ Monthly payments: $_____

Origination date: _____ Original amount: $_____

Estimated pay-off date: _____

Online username: _____ Password: _____

Debt (select one): ❏ Credit Card ❏ Student ❏ Auto ❏ Other: _____

Status: ❏ Active ❏ Grace ❏ Deferred ❏ Other: _____

Company/provider name: _____

    Contact name: _____ Phone: _____

    Address: _____

Location of documents: _____

Account number: _____ Auto pay: ❏ No ❏ Yes, amount: $ _____

Monthly due date: _____ Monthly payments: $_____

Origination date: _____ Original amount: $_____

Estimated pay-off date: _____

Online username: _____ Password: _____

Debt (select one): ❏ Credit Card ❏ Student ❏ Auto ❏ Other: _____

Status: ❏ Active ❏ Grace ❏ Deferred ❏ Other: _____

Company/provider name: _____

    Contact name: _____ Phone: _____

    Address: _____

Location of documents: _____

Account number: _____ Auto pay: ❏ No ❏ Yes, amount: $ _____

Monthly due date: _____ Monthly payments: $_____

Origination date: _____ Original amount: $_____

Estimated pay-off date: _____

Online username: _____ Password: _____

Debt (select one): ❏ Credit Card ❏ Student ❏ Auto ❏ Other: _____

Status: ❏ Active ❏ Grace ❏ Deferred ❏ Other: _____

Company/provider name: _____

    Contact name: _____ Phone: _____

    Address: _____

Location of documents: _____

Account number: _____ Auto pay: ❏ No ❏ Yes, amount: $ _____

Monthly due date: _____ Monthly payments: $_____

Origination date: _____ Original amount: $_____

Estimated pay-off date: _____

Online username: _____ Password: _____

Debt (select one): ❏ Credit Card ❏ Student ❏ Auto ❏ Other: _____

Status: ❏ Active ❏ Grace ❏ Deferred ❏ Other: _____

Company/provider name: _____

    Contact name: _____ Phone: _____

    Address: _____

Location of documents: _____

Account number: _____ Auto pay: ❏ No ❏ Yes, amount: $ _____

Monthly due date: _____ Monthly payments: $_____

Origination date: _____ Original amount: $_____

Estimated pay-off date: _____

Online username: _____ Password: _____

Debt (select one): ❏ Credit Card ❏ Student ❏ Auto ❏ Other: _____

Status: ❏ Active ❏ Grace ❏ Deferred ❏ Other: _____

Company/provider name: _____

    Contact name: _____ Phone: _____

    Address: _____

Location of documents: _____

Account number: _____ Auto pay: ❏ No ❏ Yes, amount: $ _____

Monthly due date: _____ Monthly payments: $_____

Origination date: _____ Original amount: $_____

Estimated pay-off date: _____

Online username: _____ Password: _____

Debt (select one): ❏ Credit Card ❏ Student ❏ Auto ❏ Other: _____

Status: ❏ Active ❏ Grace ❏ Deferred ❏ Other: _____

Company/provider name: _____

    Contact name: _____ Phone: _____

    Address: _____

Location of documents: _____

Account number: _____ Auto pay: ❏ No ❏ Yes, amount: $ _____

Monthly due date: _____ Monthly payments: $_____

Origination date: _____ Original amount: $_____

Estimated pay-off date: _____

Online username: _____ Password: _____

Debt (select one): ❑ Credit Card ❑ Student ❑ Auto ❑ Other: _____

Status: ❑ Active ❑ Grace ❑ Deferred ❑ Other: _____

Company/provider name: _____

    Contact name: _____ Phone: _____

    Address: _____

Location of documents: _____

Account number: _____ Auto pay: ❑ No ❑ Yes, amount: $_____

Monthly due date: _____ Monthly payments: $_____

Origination date: _____ Original amount: $_____

Estimated pay-off date: _____

Online username: _____ Password: _____

Debt (select one): ❑ Credit Card ❑ Student ❑ Auto ❑ Other: _____

Status: ❑ Active ❑ Grace ❑ Deferred ❑ Other: _____

Company/provider name: _____

    Contact name: _____ Phone: _____

    Address: _____

Location of documents: _____

Account number: _____ Auto pay: ❑ No ❑ Yes, amount: $_____

Monthly due date: _____ Monthly payments: $_____

Origination date: _____ Original amount: $_____

Estimated pay-off date: _____

Online username: _____ Password: _____

Debt (select one): ❑ Credit Card ❑ Student ❑ Auto ❑ Other: _____

Status: ❑ Active ❑ Grace ❑ Deferred ❑ Other: _____

Company/provider name: _____

    Contact name: _____ Phone: _____

    Address: _____

Location of documents: _____

Account number: _____ Auto pay: ❑ No ❑ Yes, amount: $ _____

Monthly due date: _____ Monthly payments: $_____

Origination date: _____ Original amount: $_____

Estimated pay-off date: _____

Online username: _____ Password: _____

Debt (select one): ❑ Credit Card ❑ Student ❑ Auto ❑ Other: _____

Status: ❑ Active ❑ Grace ❑ Deferred ❑ Other: _____

Company/provider name: _____

    Contact name: _____ Phone: _____

    Address: _____

Location of documents: _____

Account number: _____ Auto pay: ❑ No ❑ Yes, amount: $ _____

Monthly due date: _____ Monthly payments: $_____

Origination date: _____ Original amount: $_____

Estimated pay-off date: _____

Online username: _____ Password: _____

Debt (select one): ❏ Credit Card ❏ Student ❏ Auto ❏ Other: _____

Status: ❏ Active ❏ Grace ❏ Deferred ❏ Other: _____

Company/provider name: _____

    Contact name: _____ Phone: _____

    Address: _____

Location of documents: _____

Account number: _____ Auto pay: ❏ No ❏ Yes, amount: $ _____

Monthly due date: _____ Monthly payments: $_____

Origination date: _____ Original amount: $_____

Estimated pay-off date: _____

Online username: _____ Password: _____

Debt (select one): ❏ Credit Card ❏ Student ❏ Auto ❏ Other: _____

Status: ❏ Active ❏ Grace ❏ Deferred ❏ Other: _____

Company/provider name: _____

    Contact name: _____ Phone: _____

    Address: _____

Location of documents: _____

Account number: _____ Auto pay: ❏ No ❏ Yes, amount: $ _____

Monthly due date: _____ Monthly payments: $_____

Origination date: _____ Original amount: $_____

Estimated pay-off date: _____

Online username: _____ Password: _____

G.   Retirement Accounts and Pensions

Type (select one): ❑ 401(k) ❑ IRA ❑ Social Security ❑ Pension ❑ Other: _____

Status: (select one): ❑ Active ❑ Expired ❑ Receive payments

Location of documents: _____

Company name: _____ Contact Name: _____

Address: _____ Phone: _____

Account number: _____ Auto pay: ❑ No ❑ Yes, amount: $ _____

Type (select one): ❑ 401(k) ❑ IRA ❑ Social Security ❑ Pension ❑ Other: _____

Status: (select one): ❑ Active ❑ Expired ❑ Receive payments

Location of documents: _____

Company name: _____ Contact Name: _____

Address: _____ Phone: _____

Account number: _____ Auto pay: ❑ No ❑ Yes, amount: $ _____

Type (select one): ❑ 401(k) ❑ IRA ❑ Social Security ❑ Pension ❑ Other: _____

Status: (select one): ❑ Active ❑ Expired ❑ Receive payments

Location of documents: _____

Company name: _____ Contact Name: _____

Address: _____ Phone: _____

Account number: _____ Auto pay: ❑ No ❑ Yes, amount: $ _____

Type (select one): ❑ 401(k) ❑ IRA ❑ Social Security ❑ Pension ❑ Other: _____

Status: (select one): ❑ Active ❑ Expired ❑ Receive payments

Location of documents: _____

Company name: _____ Contact Name: _____

Address: _____ Phone: _____

Account number: _____ Auto pay: ❑ No ❑ Yes, amount: $ _____

Type (select one): ❑ 401(k) ❑ IRA ❑ Social Security ❑ Pension ❑ Other: _____

Status: (select one): ❑ Active ❑ Expired ❑ Receive payments

Location of documents: _____

Company name: _____ Contact Name: _____

Address: _____ Phone: _____

Account number: _____ Auto pay: ❑ No ❑ Yes, amount: $ _____

Type (select one): ❑ 401(k) ❑ IRA ❑ Social Security ❑ Pension ❑ Other: _____

Status: (select one): ❑ Active ❑ Expired ❑ Receive payments

Location of documents: _____

Company name: _____ Contact Name: _____

Address: _____ Phone: _____

Account number: _____ Auto pay: ❑ No ❑ Yes, amount: $ _____

Type (select one): ❑ 401(k) ❑ IRA ❑ Social Security ❑ Pension ❑ Other: _____

Status: (select one): ❑ Active ❑ Expired ❑ Receive payments

Location of documents: _____

Company name: _____ Contact Name: _____

Address: _____ Phone: _____

Account number: _____ Auto pay: ❑ No ❑ Yes, amount: $ _____

Type (select one): ❑ 401(k) ❑ IRA ❑ Social Security ❑ Pension ❑ Other: _____

Status: (select one): ❑ Active ❑ Expired ❑ Receive payments

Location of documents: _____

Company name: _____ Contact Name: _____

Address: _____ Phone: _____

Account number: _____ Auto pay: ❑ No ❑ Yes, amount: $ _____

Type (select one): ❑ 401(k) ❑ IRA ❑ Social Security ❑ Pension ❑ Other: _____

Status: (select one): ❑ Active ❑ Expired ❑ Receive payments

Location of documents: _____

Company name: _____ Contact Name: _____

Address: _____ Phone: _____

Account number: _____ Auto pay: ❑ No ❑ Yes, amount: $ _____

Type (select one): ❑ 401(k) ❑ IRA ❑ Social Security ❑ Pension ❑ Other: _____

Status: (select one): ❑ Active ❑ Expired ❑ Receive payments

Location of documents: _____

Company name: _____ Contact Name: _____

Address: _____ Phone: _____

Account number: _____ Auto pay: ❑ No ❑ Yes, amount: $ _____

Type (select one): ❑ 401(k) ❑ IRA ❑ Social Security ❑ Pension ❑ Other: _____

Status: (select one): ❑ Active ❑ Expired ❑ Receive payments

Location of documents: _____

Company name: _____ Contact Name: _____

Address: _____ Phone: _____

Account number: _____ Auto pay: ❑ No ❑ Yes, amount: $ _____

Type (select one): ❑ 401(k) ❑ IRA ❑ Social Security ❑ Pension ❑ Other: _____

Status: (select one): ❑ Active ❑ Expired ❑ Receive payments

Location of documents: _____

Company name: _____ Contact Name: _____

Address: _____ Phone: _____

Account number: _____ Auto pay: ❑ No ❑ Yes, amount: $ _____

Type (select one): ❑ 401(k) ❑ IRA ❑ Social Security ❑ Pension ❑ Other: _____

Status: (select one): ❑ Active ❑ Expired ❑ Receive payments

Location of documents: _____

Company name: _____ Contact Name: _____

Address: _____ Phone: _____

Account number: _____ Auto pay: ❑ No ❑ Yes, amount: $ _____

Type (select one): ❑ 401(k) ❑ IRA ❑ Social Security ❑ Pension ❑ Other: _____

Status: (select one): ❑ Active ❑ Expired ❑ Receive payments

Location of documents: _____

Company name: _____ Contact Name: _____

Address: _____ Phone: _____

Account number: _____ Auto pay: ❑ No ❑ Yes, amount: $ _____

Type (select one): ❑ 401(k) ❑ IRA ❑ Social Security ❑ Pension ❑ Other: _____

Status: (select one): ❑ Active ❑ Expired ❑ Receive payments

Location of documents: _____

Company name: _____ Contact Name: _____

Address: _____ Phone: _____

Account number: _____ Auto pay: ❑ No ❑ Yes, amount: $ _____

Type (select one): ❑ 401(k) ❑ IRA ❑ Social Security ❑ Pension ❑ Other: _____

Status: (select one): ❑ Active ❑ Expired ❑ Receive payments

Location of documents: _____

Company name: _____ Contact Name: _____

Address: _____ Phone: _____

Account number: _____ Auto pay: ❑ No ❑ Yes, amount: $ _____

Type (select one): ❑ 401(k) ❑ IRA ❑ Social Security ❑ Pension ❑ Other: _____

Status: (select one): ❑ Active ❑ Expired ❑ Receive payments

Location of documents: _____

Company name: _____ Contact Name: _____

Address: _____ Phone: _____

Account number: _____ Auto pay: ❑ No ❑ Yes, amount: $ _____

Type (select one): ❑ 401(k) ❑ IRA ❑ Social Security ❑ Pension ❑ Other: _____

Status: (select one): ❑ Active ❑ Expired ❑ Receive payments

Location of documents: _____

Company name: _____ Contact Name: _____

Address: _____ Phone: _____

Account number: _____ Auto pay: ❑ No ❑ Yes, amount: $ _____

Type (select one): ❑ 401(k) ❑ IRA ❑ Social Security ❑ Pension ❑ Other: _____

Status: (select one): ❑ Active ❑ Expired ❑ Receive payments

Location of documents: _____

Company name: _____ Contact Name: _____

Address: _____ Phone: _____

Account number: _____ Auto pay: ❑ No ❑ Yes, amount: $ _____

Type (select one): ❑ 401(k) ❑ IRA ❑ Social Security ❑ Pension ❑ Other: _____

Status: (select one): ❑ Active ❑ Expired ❑ Receive payments

Location of documents: _____

Company name: _____ Contact Name: _____

Address: _____ Phone: _____

Account number: _____ Auto pay: ❑ No ❑ Yes, amount: $ _____

Type (select one): ❑ 401(k) ❑ IRA ❑ Social Security ❑ Pension ❑ Other: _____

Status: (select one): ❑ Active ❑ Expired ❑ Receive payments

Location of documents: _____

Company name: _____ Contact Name: _____

Address: _____ Phone: _____

Account number: _____ Auto pay: ❑ No ❑ Yes, amount: $ _____

3. Other

A. Organ, Tissue, and Body Donation

I want to be a donor: ❏ No ❏ Yes, registered with: ❏ DMV ❏ Health department ❏ Other:

_____ ❏ Not registered, but I wish to be a donor

Donate my organs: ❏ No ❏ Yes (Only: ❏ Any organs ❏ Heart ❏ Liver ❏ Kidneys ❏ Pancreas

❏ Lungs ❏ Intestines ❏ Anything, but: _____

_____)

Donate my tissue: ❏ No ❏ Yes (Only: ❏ Any tissue ❏ Heart valves ❏ Eyes-corneas ❏ Tendons

❏ Bone ❏ Skin ❏ Veins ❏ Anything, but _____

_____)

Donate body for medical education/research: ❏ No ❏ Yes

Location of documents: _____

Arrangements made: ❏ No ❏ Yes, for _____

Organization name: _____ Phone: _____

Contact person: _____ Date arrangements made: _____

Address: _____

I want to be a donor: ❏ No ❏ Yes, registered with: ❏ DMV ❏ Health department ❏ Other:

_____ ❏ Not registered, but I wish to be a donor

Donate my organs: ❏ No ❏ Yes (Only: ❏ Any organs ❏ Heart ❏ Liver ❏ Kidneys ❏ Pancreas

❏ Lungs ❏ Intestines ❏ Anything, but: _____

_____)

Donate my tissue: ❏ No ❏ Yes (Only: ❏ Any tissue ❏ Heart valves ❏ Eyes-corneas ❏ Tendons

❏ Bone ❏ Skin ❏ Veins ❏ Anything, but _____

_____)

Donate body for medical education/research: ❏ No ❏ Yes

Location of documents: _____

Arrangements made: ❏ No ❏ Yes, for _____

Organization name: _____ Phone: _____

Contact person: _____ Date arrangements made: _____

Address: _____

I want to be a donor: ❑ No ❑ Yes, registered with: ❑ DMV ❑ Health department ❑ Other:

_____ ❑ Not registered, but I wish to be a donor

Donate my organs: ❑ No ❑ Yes (Only: ❑ Any organs ❑ Heart ❑ Liver ❑ Kidneys ❑ Pancreas

❑ Lungs ❑ Intestines ❑ Anything, but: _____

_____)

Donate my tissue: ❑ No ❑ Yes (Only: ❑ Any tissue ❑ Heart valves ❑ Eyes-corneas ❑ Tendons

❑ Bone ❑ Skin ❑ Veins ❑ Anything, but _____

_____)

Donate body for medical education/research: ❑ No ❑ Yes

Location of documents: _____

Arrangements made: ❑ No ❑ Yes, for _____

Organization name: _____ Phone: _____

Contact person: _____ Date arrangements made: _____

Address: _____

B. Inform the World of Your Death
a) Cremation or Burial, and Funeral and Memorial Services

Cremation or Burial (select one)

❑ Cremated (❑ Columbarium niche ❑ In the ground ❑ Scattered over: _____

_____

    ❑ Ashes to, name: _____ Phone: _____

       Address: _____

    ❑ Urn: ❑ No ❑ Yes, type: ❑ Ceramic ❑ Stone: _____

       ❑ Other: _____

       Budget: $_____ at least: $_____ ❑ No budget)

[OR]

❑ Buried (❑ Below ground ❑ Above ground) Plot location: _____

_____

    Burial marker: ❑ No ❑ Yes, budget: ❑ $_____ at least: $_____ ❑ Any

      Size: ❑ Any ❑ Same size as neighbors' ❑ Large

      Statue material: ❑ Any ❑ Stone: _____

       ❑ Other: _____

      Design: ❑ Any ❑ _____

_____

      Epitaph: ❑ No ❑ Yes, inscription: _____

_____

_____

    Casket: budget: Stay Under: $_____ At least: $_____ ❑ Any

Material: ❑ Any ❑ Wood: _____

❑ Other: _____

Exterior Finish and Design: ❑ Any ❑ Other: _____

_____

_____)

Arrangements made: ❑ No ❑ Yes, for: _____

Funeral home name: _____ Phone: _____

Contact person: _____ Date arrangements made: _____

Address: _____

Location of documents: _____

Time of cremation/burial (select one): ❑ After service ❑ Before service ❑ Immediately after I die
Embalm (select one): ❑ No ❑ Yes ❑ No preference
Attire to be cremated/buried in (select one): ❑ Traditional ❑ Any ❑ As follows: _____

_____

_____

Funeral and Memorial Services

Type of service: ❑ Religious ❑ Military ❑ Other: _____
❑ Open to the public ❑ Wake ❑ Open casket ❑ Body present ❑ Flowers ❑ Photograph
displayed ❑ Photograph location: _____ ❑ No preference

Budget: $_____   At least: $_____   ❑ Any
Time preference: ❑ Morning ❑ Afternoon   ❑ Evening ❑ Day preference: _____
Attire during service: ❑ Any ❑ Traditional ❑ Same as cremation/buried ❑ As follows: _____

_____

_____

Specific request(s): _____

_____

Arrangements made: ❏ No ❏ Yes, for: _____

    Funeral home name: _____ Phone: _____

    Contact person: _____ Date arrangements made: _____

    Address: _____

    Location of documents: _____

Eulogy

Eulogizer name: _____ Phone: _____

    Address: _____

Eulogizer name: _____ Phone: _____

    Address: _____

Eulogizer name: _____ Phone: _____

    Address: _____

Readings

Name: _____ Phone: _____

    Address: _____

Name: _____ Phone: _____

    Address: _____

Name: _____ Phone: _____

    Address: _____

Reception

Arrangements made: ❏ No ❏ Yes, for _____

    Organization name: _____ Phone: _____

    Contact person: _____ Date arrangements made: _____

Address: _____

Location of documents: _____

Immediately following funeral/memorial service: ❑ No ❑ Yes, then: _____

Budget: $_____   At least: $_____   ❑ Any

Time preference: ❑ Morning ❑ Afternoon ❑ Evening ❑ Day preference: _____

Specific request(s): _____

Type of reception: ❑ Religious ❑ Military ❑ Other: _____ ❑ Open to the
    public ❑ Wake ❑ Open casket ❑ Body present ❑ Flowers ❑ Photograph displayed
    ❑ Photograph location: _____ ❑ No preference

Food and Drinks: _____

_____

_____

_____

_____

_____

_____

Specific requests: _____

_____

_____

_____

Pallbearers and Alternate Pallbearers

❑ Pallbearer ❑ Alternate pallbearer ❑ Either

    Name: _____ Phone: _____

    Address: _____

❑ Pallbearer ❑ Alternate pallbearer ❑ Either

    Name: _____ Phone: _____

    Address: _____

❑ Pallbearer ❑ Alternate pallbearer ❑ Either

    Name: _____ Phone: _____

    Address: _____

❑ Pallbearer ❑ Alternate pallbearer ❑ Either

    Name: _____ Phone: _____

    Address: _____

❑ Pallbearer ❑ Alternate pallbearer ❑ Either

    Name: _____ Phone: _____

    Address: _____

❑ Pallbearer ❑ Alternate pallbearer ❑ Either

    Name: _____ Phone: _____

    Address: _____

❑ Pallbearer ❑ Alternate pallbearer ❑ Either

    Name: _____ Phone: _____

    Address: _____

❑ Pallbearer ❑ Alternate pallbearer ❑ Either

    Name: _____ Phone: _____

    Address: _____

❑ Pallbearer ❑ Alternate pallbearer ❑ Either

    Name: _____ Phone: _____

    Address: _____

❑ Pallbearer ❑ Alternate pallbearer ❑ Either

    Name: _____ Phone: _____

    Address: _____

❑ Pallbearer ❑ Alternate pallbearer ❑ Either

    Name: _____ Phone: _____

    Address: _____

❑ Pallbearer ❑ Alternate pallbearer ❑ Either

    Name: _____ Phone: _____

    Address: _____

❑ Pallbearer ❑ Alternate pallbearer ❑ Either

    Name: _____ Phone: _____

    Address: _____

❑ Pallbearer ❑ Alternate pallbearer ❑ Either

    Name: _____ Phone: _____

    Address: _____

❑ Pallbearer ❑ Alternate pallbearer ❑ Either

Name: _____ Phone: _____

Address: _____

❑ Pallbearer ❑ Alternate pallbearer ❑ Either

Name: _____ Phone: _____

Address: _____

❑ Pallbearer ❑ Alternate pallbearer ❑ Either

Name: _____ Phone: _____

Address: _____

❑ Pallbearer ❑ Alternate pallbearer ❑ Either

Name: _____ Phone: _____

Address: _____

❑ Pallbearer ❑ Alternate pallbearer ❑ Either

Name: _____ Phone: _____

Address: _____

❑ Pallbearer ❑ Alternate pallbearer ❑ Either

Name: _____ Phone: _____

Address: _____

❑ Pallbearer ❑ Alternate pallbearer ❑ Either

Name: _____ Phone: _____

Address: _____

❑ Pallbearer ❑ Alternate pallbearer ❑ Either

    Name: _____ Phone: _____

    Address: _____

❑ Pallbearer ❑ Alternate pallbearer ❑ Either

    Name: _____ Phone: _____

    Address: _____

❑ Pallbearer ❑ Alternate pallbearer ❑ Either

    Name: _____ Phone: _____

    Address: _____

❑ Pallbearer ❑ Alternate pallbearer ❑ Either

    Name: _____ Phone: _____

    Address: _____

❑ Pallbearer ❑ Alternate pallbearer ❑ Either

    Name: _____ Phone: _____

    Address: _____

❑ Pallbearer ❑ Alternate pallbearer ❑ Either

    Name: _____ Phone: _____

    Address: _____

❑ Pallbearer ❑ Alternate pallbearer ❑ Either

    Name: _____ Phone: _____

    Address: _____

❏ Pallbearer ❏ Alternate pallbearer ❏ Either

    Name: _____ Phone: _____

    Address: _____

❏ Pallbearer ❏ Alternate pallbearer ❏ Either

    Name: _____ Phone: _____

    Address: _____

❏ Pallbearer ❏ Alternate pallbearer ❏ Either

    Name: _____ Phone: _____

    Address: _____

❏ Pallbearer ❏ Alternate pallbearer ❏ Either

    Name: _____ Phone: _____

    Address: _____

❏ Pallbearer ❏ Alternate pallbearer ❏ Either

    Name: _____ Phone: _____

    Address: _____

❏ Pallbearer ❏ Alternate pallbearer ❏ Either

    Name: _____ Phone: _____

    Address: _____

❏ Pallbearer ❏ Alternate pallbearer ❏ Either

    Name: _____ Phone: _____

    Address: _____

b)   Newspaper Obituary Information

I want my obituary published: ❑ No ❑ Yes, in the following publication(s): _____

_____

I have drafted a version: ❑ No ❑ Yes (see below)
The final version should be written by:

Name: _____ Phone: _____

Address: _____

I want a photograph included: ❑ No ❑ Yes, ❑ enclosed is the photo

Obituary Information

Name:	
Place of Birth:	
City:	
DOB:	
Spouse, children, grand-children, etc.:	
Military service:	
Organization and/or houses of worship mem-bership:	
Employment:	
Achievements:	
Education:	
Hobbies:	
Services Place Name and Address:	
Services date/time:	
Service conducted by:	
Flowers:	❑ Yes. Send To: ❑ No flowers ❑ But remembrance donations to:
Donations:	
Additional notes:	

C. Other Notes

Best Selling Titles

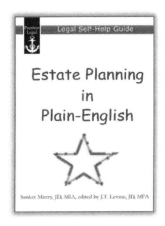

Made in the USA
Las Vegas, NV
16 May 2021